Fostering Entrepreneurial Success
(Prosperity through Innovation)

Fostering Entrepreneurial Success

(Prosperity through Innovation)

Dr. Sanjeev Chaturvedi
Dr. Dibyendu Choudhury
Dr. Shreekant Sharma

GYAN
ni-msme

Published, 2018

Published by

Gyan Publishing House
5, Ansari Road
Daryaganj, New Delhi-110002
Phone: 011-47034999, 9811692060
www.gyanbooks.com
E-mail: books@gyanbooks.com

National Institute for Micro, Small and Medium Enterprises (ni-msme)
(An Organisation of the Ministry of MSME, Govt. of India)
Yousufguda, Hyderabad-500045,
Telangana, India

Printed at: G. Print Process, Delhi.

Cataloging in Publication Data—DK
Courtesy: D.K. Agencies (P) Ltd. <docinfo@dkagencies.com>

Fostering entrepreneurial success : prosperity through innovation / [editors],
Dr. Sanjeev Chaturvedi, Dr. Dibyendu Choudhury, Dr. Shreekant Sharma.
pages cm
Contributed articles.
Includes bibliographical references.
ISBN 9788121214483

1. Entrepreneurship—India. 2. Small business—India. 3. Technological innovations—India. 4. Success in business—India. I. Chaturvedi, Sanjeev, editor. II. Choudhury, Dibyendu, editor. III. Sharma, Shreekant, editor.

LCC HB615.F67 2018 | DDC 338.040954 23

Contents

PREFACE

"I see start-ups, technology and innovation as exciting and effective instruments for India's transformation".

NARENDRA MODI,
PRIME MINISTER OF INDIA

Many researchers around the world have believed, entrepreneurship to be catalyst for economic growth and an antidote to unemployment. It has been proposed that entrepreneurship can be a panacea for empowerment, job creation, economic transformation, and poverty reduction, particularly in India. Entrepreneurship has been described as the "capacity and willingness to develop, organize and manage a business venture along with any of its risks in order to make profit.

The Government of India and Various State Governments have made remarkabale endeavours to develop an entrepreneurial supportive eco-system in the country. The Ministry of Micro, Small & Medium Enterprises and its organizations are assisting the States in their efforts to encourage entrepreneurship, employment and livelihood opportunities and enhance the competitiveness of MSMEs in the changed economic scenario. Ministry of MSME envisions a vibrant MSME sector by promoting growth and development of the MSME Sector.

Entrepreneurship has become the engine of industrial development in all the developing countries including India. Economic development of a nation mainly relies on the industrialisation. Industrialisation helps solve the various socio-economic problems encountered by the developing countries. But these economies do not have adequate resources to build a strong industrial base by setting up large scale industries. They have to depend on small scale sector for the speedy development of their economies. Promotion of entrepreneurship is the most popular aim of Indian policy makers in present times. Rising population on the one hand and lack of employment opportunities on the other point to the need for entrepreneurship promotion. An entrepreneur is a person who has possession over a new enterprise or venture and assumes full accountability for the inherent risks and the outcome. Some observers see them as willing to accept a high level of personal, professional or financial risk to pursue that opportunity. A commonly accepted description of entrepreneurship is "a process of identifying, evaluating and seizing an opportunity, and bringing together all the resources necessary for its success, by devoting time and effort".

In common perception it is taken for granted that entrepreneurs driven by some internal motivation simply emerge. But, little is known about the amount of obstacles they face at the inception stage. These include self-confidence, raising start-up finance, lack of information/advice on how to start a business, difficult to find right contacts for business, no awareness/ access to business support, lacked management skills, lacked entrepreneurial skills, lacked inter-cultural and language skills for foreign markets, difficulty in combining family and work life balance. Even though entrepreneurship is a personal process, success and failure are likely to be partially dictated by personality, by better understanding the skills, traits, and behaviours that shape the thought process.

Innovation is simply "a new way of doing something". As a discipline, innovation is capable of being learned, as well as practiced. Innovation consists of the purposeful and organised search for changes and in the systematic analysis of the opportunities such changes might offer for economic or social innovation. Social entrepreneurship as a career choice has social well being as a distinct driver of motivation. In one direction the entrepreneur is aggrandizing wealth for self and in the other the entrepreneur is sacrificing for the common good.

Start-up India, as outlined in the Action Plan, refers to promotion of innovative enterprises with considerable extent of research and development carried out in collaboration with higher educational and scientific research institutions. Technology Business Incubators promoted for this purpose are normally established in collaboration with a host of leading higher educational and scientific research institutions. Linking industry with academia to focus on new areas that have potential for development is the direction planned to be pursued for encouraging start- up entities in various sectors. To facilitate the youth to take up innovative ventures, creating a favourable and liberal eco system is a pre-requisite. Easier entry and faster exit are emphasised for the success of these enterprises which involve high risk. In such programmes, the key players that deserve special mention are Ministry of MSME, Ministry of Skill Development and

Entrepreneurship, Department of Science and Technology (DST), Department of Industrial Policy and Promotion, Small Industries Development Bank of India (SIDBI) etc.

Beside this it is important to bring prosperity to rural areas, agripreneurship have the potential to contribute to a range of social and economic development such as employment generation, income generation, poverty reduction and improvements in nutrition, health and overall food security in the national economy.

We thank the contributors and wish the readers to make best use of the published research works for developing a thriving entrepreneurial eco-system.

Best Wishes,

Dr. Sanjeev Chaturvedi
Dr. Dibyendu Choudhury
Dr. Shreekant Sharma

LIST OF CONTRIBUTORS

1. **Dr. Meghna Chhabra,** Faculty in Management & Commerce, K. R. Mangalam University, Gurgaon.
2. **Dr. Yamini Karmarkar,** Associate Professor in Management Programs of International Institute of Professional Studies, Devi Ahilya University, Indore.
3. **Mr. V. Padmanand,** Director and Mr. Kunal Sood is partner, Grant Thornton (GT) LLP.
4. **Mr. M. Chandrashekar Reddy,** Former-Director General, ni-msme, Hyderabad.
5. **Dr. D. Nagayya,** Consultant on Small and Medium Enterprises, Guntur; and Former Director (Industrial Development), National Institute for Micro, Small and Medium Enterprises (ni-msme), Hyderabad
6. **Dr. Balla Appa Rao,** UGC Emeritus Professor, Ex-Dean and Head, Dept. of Commerce and Management Studies, Andhra University, Visakhapatnam-530003 (Andhra Pradesh).
7. **Dr. Dipanjan Chakraborty,** Associate Professor, Department of Commerce, Darrang College, Tezpur, Assam.
8. **Ms. Pom Sen Chakraborty,** Assistant Professor, Department of Commerce, Darrang College, Tezpur, Assam.
9. **Mr. Regalla Ravikanth,** Research Scholar, Board of Studies, School of Management Studies, JNTU, Hyderabad- 500085.
10. **Dr. M.S. Bhat,** Ph.D. Supervisor, Director (Retd.) Board of Studies, School of Management Studies, JNTU, Hyderabad- 500085.
11. **Dr. D. Ragunatha Reddy,** Ph.D Co-Supervisor, Professor and Chairman, Board of Studies, School of Management Studies, JNTU, Hyderabad- 500085.
12. **Dr. T. Mohamed Ilyas,** Associate Professor of Commerce, Islamiah College, Vaniyambadi-635 751, Tamil Nadu.

13. **Dr. Resmi Ann Thomas,** Assistant Professor, Institute of Public Enterprise, Hyderabad-500007.
14. **Dr. T.J. Kamalanabhan,** Professor, Department of Management Studies, Indian Institute of Technology, Madras, Chennai-600036.
15. **Dr. Anil Kumar,** Associate Professor, Haryana School of Business, Guru Jambheshwar University of Science & Technology, Hisar-125001 (Haryana).
16. **Dr. Girija Nandini,** Asst. Professor, Department of Management Studies, Regional College of Management, Bhubaneswar, Odisha.
17. **Dr. Vivek Sharma,** Consultant, Centre for Good Governance & Administrative Reforms, Institute of Management, Public Administration and Rural Development, Main Campus, Srinagar, M. A. Road, Srinagar (Kashmir).
18. **Dr. Sudhir K. Jain,** Retd. Professor and Head, Department of Management Studies, Indian Institute of Technology, Hauz Khas, New Delhi-110016.
19. **Dr. Brajaballav Kar,** Associate Professor, Operations Management, School of Management, KIIT University, Bhubaneswar, Odisha.
20. **Mr. Sushree Ranjan Tripathy** is entrepreneur and Partner Venus Leather, Odisha.
21. **Dr. B.S.V. Meera Setty,** Assistant Professor & HOD, Mahatama Gandhi Govt. College, Mayabunder, North Andaman-744204, Andaman & Nicobar Islands.

List of Tables

LIST OF FIGURES

1

Entrepreneur Generation and Entrepreneurial Success - An Empirical Study

— *T. Mohamed Ilyas*

Entrepreneurship has become the engine of industrial development in all the developing countries including India. Several researchers have conducted studies on the socio-economic background of entrepreneurs and determinants of entrepreneurship. They have analysed factors responsible for entrepreneurship development. Studies on quantifiable variables such as return on investment, capacity utilisation, turnover, and number of workers employed are frequently carried out. But studies on classification of entrepreneurs into very much successful, successful, or unsuccessful are scarce.

In India, M.M.P. Akhouri (1978) was the first to develop a mathematical model for assessing entrepreneurial success. This composite method of measuring entrepreneurial success was later applied to different countries like Bangladesh and Korea. The Entrepreneurial Economic Success Index (EESI) of Akhouri was said to be a composite method of measuring entrepreneurial success in the sense that it includes the methods of both economists and behaviourists.

The economists generally consider the economic ratios like profit per unit capital, employment per unit investment, production rate, and growth rate over a period of time for measuring entrepreneurial success. Behaviourists like McClelland and Winter (1969) consider psychological factors like the idea of starting new ventures, risk taking ability, longer working hours, and responsibility as different parameters for measuring entrepreneurial success. Neither the economists, nor the behaviourists could suggest a common method of measuring the success status of an entrepreneur. In 1979 Akhouri had filled the gap by developing the comprehensive model, including both economists and behaviourists methods, which is known as EESI.

The researcher has attempted in the present study by applying the Akhouri EESI to classify the leather industry entrepreneurs into 'Very Successful', 'Successful', and 'Unsuccessful' categories.

Akhouri EESI has four behavioral dimensions which are adequately represented by economic activities. They are outline below.

(1) The first dimension of EESI is the propensity to take risk in the entrepreneur. This can very well be represented by the entrepreneur's ability to invest his own capital. This can be judged with the proportion of the entrepreneur's own capital invested to the total of his own capacity to invest.

(2) The second dimension of EESI is the ability of the entrepreneur to sense and mobilise resources for attaining their goal: the capacity of an entrepreneur to borrow or raise capital from other sources such as family, friends and other financial institutions. This dimension reveals the ability of entrepreneurs to borrow or raise capital to achieve their goal.

(3) The third dimension of the EESI is related to the managerial efficiency of the entrepreneur. The amount of profit per unit investment is a fair indicator of managerial efficiency. Hence the percentage of net profit after taxes and interest on total investment is considered necessary in this dimension.

(4) The last dimension of the EESI is the farsightedness of the entrepreneur in terms of future progress and growth. The ability to strive for progress and further growth is a fair indicator for continuous survival and success. Hence for this dimension, the proportion of total profit re-invested for further expansion, diversification, modernisation, etc., is taken into account by Akhouri.

The above four indicators no doubt consider both economic activities and psychological aspects of the entrepreneurs. By combining these four indicators, Akhouri has developed the mathematical model known as EESI which classifies entrepreneurs into three categories namely, Very Successful, Successful, and Un successful. To measure the propensity of risk taken by the entrepreneurs, Akhouri has adopted the tool of finding the ratio between own capital (OC) and the capacity to raise and invest capital (OCTY). To measure the second feature the technique he has adopted is the summation of the proportion of total investment come as borrowed capital (BC) and raised capital (RC), i.e., $\frac{\text{BC}}{\text{TI}}$ of BC + $\frac{\text{BC}}{\text{TI}}$ of RC.

The managerial efficiency is measured in terms of net profit (NP) generated per unit of investment, i.e., $\frac{\text{NP}}{\text{TI}}$ The last feature of the quality of constantly striving for progress and further growth is equated by the proportion of net profit re-invested (PR) for progress and further growth, i.e., $\frac{\text{PR}}{\text{NP}}$.

With the help of the above four different indicators, Akhouri has developed his mathematical model as shown below:

$$\text{EESI} = \frac{\text{WTI}}{\text{TI}} \quad \frac{NP}{TI} \quad \frac{PR}{NP}$$

$$\text{Where WTI} \quad \frac{OC}{OCTY}\text{of OC} \quad \frac{BC}{IT}\text{of BC} \quad \frac{RC}{TI}\text{of RC}$$

$$\text{WTI} \quad \frac{OC^2}{OCTY} \quad \frac{BC^2}{TI} \quad \frac{RC^2}{T}$$

OCTY= Own capacity to invest; OC= Own capital

BC= Borrowed capital; RC= Raised capital

TI= Total investment; NP= Net profit

PR= Profit reinvested.

Objectives and methodology

This study has been attempted with the main objective of determining the success status of leather industry entrepreneurs of Vellore district of Tamil Nadu. According to the Association of Tanners of four important dominating towns of Vellore district where leather industries are situated namely, Vaniyambadi, Ambur, Pernambut and Ranipet, there are 550 leather industries. The list of leather industries was obtained from the Tanners Association of these four towns. From each town or strata a quota of fifteen leather industries was identified to collect the data. The fifteen leather industries were selected by using random numbers. Therefore the total number of sample was 60 and hence the sampling design used was purposive, stratified, disproportionate random sampling. All the sample respondents are male only. A self-styled questionnaire-cum- interview schedule was prepared to gather relevant information so as to classify the respondent entrepreneur as first generation or second generation entrepreneur. By applying Akhouri's index they were classified into three categories as Very much Successful, Successful, and Unsuccessful.

Entrepreneurial Economic Success

Index

The researcher has applied the Akhouri EESI to determine the success status among the leather industry entrepreneurs. The same cut-off value as fixed by Akhouri under Indian conditions, as given below, was applied by the researcher in the present study.

Table - 1.1: Success status of entrepreneurs under Indian conditions

Very successful entrepreneur	*Successful entrepreneur*	*Unsuccessful entrepreneur*
1. Who invests at least 60% of his capacity to invest as own capital	Who invests 50% of his own	Who invests less than 50% of his capacity to invest as own capital
2. Can borrow or raise 8 times more capital than own capital	Can borrow or raise capital at least equal to his own capital	Can borrow or raise capital less than his own capital
3. Can make a net profit (after tax & interest) of 20% of Total Investment	Can make a net profit (after tax & interest) of 10% of Total Investment	Can make net profit after tax & interest) of less than 10% of Total Investment
4. Reinvests at least 25% of the net profit for progress and further growth	Reinvests at least 20% of his net profit for progress and further growth	Reinvests less than 20% of his net profit for progress and further growth
Index value = 0.4 or above	0.2 or above but less than 0.4	less than 0.2

Town-wise success status of leather industry entrepreneurs

By applying Akhouri's index with the same cut-off-value, the author was able to classify the sample entrepreneurs based on their success status. The following table provides the number and percentage of entrepreneurs who are classified as Very Successful, Successful, and Unsuccessful.

Table - 1.2: Town-wise success status of leather industry entrepreneurs

Town	*Success Status*			*Total*
	Very Successful	*Successful*	*Unsuccessful*	
Ambur	6 (40)	6 (40)	3 (20)	15 (100)
Vaniyambadi	4 (27)	5 (33)	6 (40)	15 (100)
Pernambut	2 (13)	3 (20)	10 (67)	15 (100)
Ranipet	5 (33)	4 (27)	6 (40)	15 (100)
Total	**17 (28.3)**	**18 (30.0)**	**25 (41.7)**	**60 (100)**

Source: Survey data.

Note: Figures in parentheses are percentages to row total.

It is worthwhile to note that 28.3 per cent of the total sample entrepreneurs have been classified as 'Very Successful' as per the EESI cut-off value, i.e., 0.4 and above. Thirty per cent of the sample was classified as 'Successful' since they obtained the cut-off value between 0.2 and 0.4. More than 40 per cent of the sample was classified as 'Unsuccessful' since their score was less than 0.2.

The above analysis also reveals the entrepreneurs' success status town- wise. Forty per cent of the entrepreneurs who belonged to Ambur town were very successful, which is followed by Ranipet with 33 per cent. Twenty-seven per cent of the Vaniyambadi entrepreneurs were very successful, whereas they were just 13 per cent in Pernambut town.

More than one-third (40%) of the entrepreneurs belonging to Ambur town were classified as Successful. Exactly one-third of the entrepreneurs belonging to Vaniyambadi town happened to be successful. Twenty-seven per cent of the Ranipet entrepreneurs appeared to be successful whereas they were just twenty per cent among the Pernambut entrepreneurs.

When 'Unsuccessful' status among the sample entrepreneurs is compared, it is important to note that two-thirds of Pernambut entrepreneurs were classified as Unsuccessful. The share of the unsuccessful among the Vaniyambadi and Ranipet entrepreneurs were forty per cent each. Only in Ambur town rate of the unsuccessful was 20 per cent, which is the lowest among all the four towns.

Success status among two generations of entrepreneurs

As this study is related to two generations of entrepreneurs, it is essential to define first generation and second generation entrepreneurs.

First generation entrepreneurs are defined as those persons who do not possess the family business background and venture into the business optionally and autonomously, whereas second generation entrepreneurs are persons who hail from the same family and inherit business legacy through familial links in terms of tangible and intangible assets, as well as the appropriate environment and expertise at young age.

From the data collected with the help of the questionnaire-cum-interview schedule, the author was able to classify 24 respondents as belonging to first generation and 36 respondents as belonging to second generation category.

The success status of both categories of entrepreneurs is indicated mentioned below in table-1.3.

Table - 1.3: Success status of first and second generations of entrepreneurs

Entrepreneur generation	*Success Status*			*Total*
	Very Successful	*Successful*	*Unsuccessful*	
First	11 (45.8)	8 (33.3)	5 (20.8)	24 (100)
Second	6 (16.7)	10 (27.8)	20 (55.6)	36 (100)
Total	**17 (28.3)**	**18 (30.0)**	**25 (41.7)**	**60 (100)**

Source: Survey data.
Note: Figures in parentheses are percentages to row total.

The table reveals that nearly half (45.8%) of the first generation entrepreneurs were very successful and similarly one-third (33.3%) of them were successful. The percentage of unsuccessful entrepreneurs among the first generation entrepreneurs was very low at 20.8 per cent.

The success status among the second generation reveals that one-sixth of them (16.7%) have been very successful. More than one-fourth (27.8%) of them turned out to be successful, whereas more than half (55.6%) were identified as unsuccessful.

Relationship between entrepreneur generation and success level

The analytical table-1.2 reveals that the success rate among the first generation entrepreneurs was more than three-fourth (i.e., 45.8% Very Successful and 33.3% Successful), whereas it was less than half (i.e.,

16.7% Very Successful and 27.8% successful) among the second generation entrepreneurs.

The ratio of unsuccessful entrepreneurs was 1:2.67 between first and second generation entrepreneurs. Hence it may concluded that the entrepreneurial success is higer among the first generation entrepreneurs than the second generation entrepreneurs.

Conclusion

The promotion of SMEs and their success are regarded as a means for enabling the local population to participate actively in the country's economic and social development. The SMEs in India have assumed a significant role in industrialisation, employment generation and economic development. The leather industry has significantly contributed to the nation's economic development and is earning sufficient foreign exchange by exporting finished leather and leather products. The success level of leather industry entrepreneurs determined in this study is expected to provide the future entrepreneurs who want to invest in leather industry with relevant insights. This is desirable as it has been proved in this study that first generation entrepreneurs' success rate is higher than that of second generation entrepreneurs. Though the Government is not granting permission for starting fresh tanneries because of effluence problem, the existing tanneries may be taken on lease by the first generation entrepreneurs so that the existing industries may be further developed.

2

ENTREPRENEURS IN SMALL SCALE SECTOR: A STUDY OF INFRASTRUCTURAL BARRIERS

—*ANIL KUMAR*

Introduction

Economic development of a nation mainly relies on the industrialisation. Industrialisation helps solve the various socio-economic problems encountered by the developing countries. But these economies do not have adequate resources to build a strong industrial base by setting up large scale industries. They have to depend on small scale sector for the speedy development of their economies. Moreover, they lack a strong human capital base, and whatever manpower is available in the country can be better utilised in the small scale sector. The problem of poverty, inequality and unbalanced regional development can be abridged by the expansion of small scale units. This sector contributes towards the country's exports and helps solve the problem of balance of payments of the economy.

Small scale sector maintains better rapport between the employer and the employees, thereby maintaining better industrial relations. The sector requires less capital as compared to large scale units, and unit can be started by the new generation of entrepreneurs. It can act as a nursery of entrepreneurship in the developing economies. Keeping in view the significance of small scale sector, an attempt has been made in this paper to analyse the infrastructure related problems faced by the small entrepreneurs, which become more imperative in the era of free markets, where efficiency is the way of life. This area needs intensive study because infrastructure related problems can not be tackled by individual entrepreneurs. Without strong infrastructure, the industry cannot move in the right direction. The state has to provide strong infrastructure in the form of transportation, energy, technology and financial institutions to fulfill the basic requirements of the small scale sector.

Review of literature

The literature contains various studies conducted in this area. Some of them are discussed in the following paragraphs.

Taylor and Brooksbank (1995) examined the marketing practices among small New Zealand organisations by taking a sample of 427 small business owners. Their findings revealed that the small business firms look at the marketing practices differently from their larger counterparts. Small business owners use marketing practices according to their financial capacity and sometimes they resort to word-of-mouth methods.

Mambula (2002) analysed the major constraints faced by the SMEs in Nigeria. A sample of 32 small business entrepreneurs was taken. The analysis of data revealed that majority of the SMEs faced the problem of finance and infrastructure while managing their businesses. The author recommended that small business entrepreneurs should collaborate with each other to sort out the various problems faced by them. There is a need to form an alliance of the Government, research institutions and financial institutions to create appropriate training for prospective small businesses. All these measures will go a long way to strengthen the growth of small scale sector.

Alagappan and Nagammai (2003) have examined the entrepreneurs' perception of financial institutions. A sample of 120 SSI units was selected from Madurai district. The study showed that the entrepreneurs had average level of satisfaction with the lending practices of financial institutions. The reason for this was attributed to larger margin money requirement and higher service charges taken by them. The authors suggested various measures to remove all these hurdles for speedy growth of entrepreneurship in SSI sector. It was also observed that financial and supporting measures were essential for the growth of small scale sector.

Dagar (2003) has examined the industrial relations in small scale sector by taking a sample of 50 SSI units from the NCR region of Delhi. The study highlighted that better facilities for employees would help maintain better industrial relations among the SSI units, and suggested following effective HR policies to reduce labour turnover in small scale sector.

Tagoe et al. (2005) have examined the financial challenges faced by the urban SMEs under financial sector liberalisation in Ghana. The main challenge was access to affordable credit over a reasonable period. To manage this challenge, the SMEs should keep records in an effective manner. Moreover, availability of collateral improves the SMEs'access to formal credit. But better availability of investment avenues further reduces the accessibility of credit to SMEs.

Kuruba (2006) has examined the issues in the promotion of small business enterprises in Botswana, and observed that Botswana economy had atmosphere congenial for the growth of small business enterprises. There is a need to provide training, and financial and institutional support for these enterprises.

Dubey and Shukla (2007) have examined various issues and challenges faced by SSIs under the WTO regime. The study has suggested that there should be easy accessibility of technology to this sector. R & D at local level should be encouraged. There should be co-ordination between Government, industry and institutes of higher learning in this direction. The technology development fund should be further strengthened in this direction.

Ismail et al. (2006) have examined motivation in business start-up among the Malay entrepreneurs and the problems faced by them. The study has concluded that there were a large number of motivational factors, but chief among them were personal development and financial security. Insufficient finance and tough competition from others were the main problems faced by the entrepreneurs.

Wu et al. (2008) have examined the empirical evidence of small business financing in China. A sample of 60 small businesses from three cities of China was taken. The study revealed that at the initial stage, these SMEs had used own sources and finances from relatives and friends. But at the later stages, they had used bank finance. The reason was, banks in China required various formalities to be fulfilled by the SMEs such as taxation submission reports, accounting and credit rating scores, documentation, etc.

The above studies have touched upon various aspects relating to small scale entrepreneurs but none of the studies had touched the area of infrastructural constraints. The present study proposes to fill this gap.

Objectives

The study was pursued with the objective of examining and analysing the infrastructural problems faced by the small scale entrepreneurs in five areas, as stated below.

- technological changes
- taking loans from financial institutions
- transportation
- frequent breakdown of power
- getting information

Methodology

To achieve the objective, a sample of 160 entrepreneurs was taken from two states of northern India: Haryana and Punjab. To analyse the various infrastructure related problems faced by the entrepreneurs, a Likert type five-degree scale ranging from 'to a great extent' to 'not at all' was developed. However, with respect to problems relating to technological changes (table-2.1) and problems relating to frequent power breakdown (table-2.4), responses were obtained for four points and three points of the scale only.

The chi-square statistic was used to decide the significance of association between factors. A well designed questionnaire was administered to the sample entrepreneurs. Five questions were asked and five statements were administered to the entrepreneurs. They were regarding the —

1. Extent of problem of technological changes
2. Extent of problem of taking loans from financial institutions
3. Extent of problem of transportation
4. Extent of problem of getting information
5. Extent of problem of frequent power breakdown

Hypotheses

The study is based on the following null hypotheses:

H_1: There is no association between the age of entrepreneurs and the problem of technological change.

H_2: There is no association between the education of entrepreneurs and the problem of technological change.

H_3: There is no association between the occupational background of the entrepreneurs and problem of technological change.

H_4: There is no association between the age of entrepreneurs and the problem of taking loans from financial institutions.

H_5: There is no association between the education of entrepreneurs and the problem of taking loans from financial institutions.

H_6: There is no association between the occupational background of entrepreneurs and the problem of taking loans from financial institutions.

H_7: There is no association between the age of entrepreneurs and the problem of transportation.

H_8: There is no association between the education of entrepreneurs and the problem of transportation.

H_9: There is no association between the occupational background of entrepreneurs and the problem of transportation.

H_{10} : There is no association between the age of entrepreneurs and the problem of frequent power breakdown.

H_{11}: There is no association between the education of entrepreneurs and the problem of frequent power breakdown.

H_{12}: There is no association between the occupational background of entrepreneurs and the problem of frequent power breakdown.

H_{13}: There is no association between the age of entrepreneurs and the problem of getting information.

H_{14}: There is no association between the education of entrepreneurs and the problem of getting information.

H_{15}: There is no association between the occupational background of entrepreneurs and the problem of getting information.

Results and discussion

In the era of globalisation, the significance of technological changes has assumed greater significance. The efficiency of the business, to a large extent, is influenced by the adoption of technological innovations, which help reduce the cost of production and price of the commodity — important in the present scenario. The data in table-2.1 shows the extent of the problem of technological innovations faced by the sample entrepreneurs.

Table - 2.1: Problems relating to technological changes

Group	*To a great extent*	*To a large extent*	*To some extent*	*To little extent*
All data	38 (.23.8)	52 (32.5)	56 (35.0)	14 (8.8)
Age (years)				
Less than 35	8 (30.8)	2 (7..7)	10 (38.5)	6 (23.1)
35 to 40	8 (25.0)	10 (31.3)	12 (37.5)	2 (6.3)
40-45	6 (14.3)	24 (57.1)	10 (23.8)	2 (4.8)
45-50	4 (18.2)	10 (45.5)	8 (36.4)	-
50+	12 (31.6)	6 (15.8)	16 (42.1)	4 (10.5)
Chi-square = 31.962	df=12	Significant at 5 per cent level		
Education				
Schooling	16 (26.7)	14 (23.3)	26 (43.3)	4 (6.7)
Graduate	12 (16.2)	32 (43.2)	22 (29.2)	8 (10.8)
Post-graduate	10 (38.5)	6 (23.1)	8 (30.8)	2 (7.7)
Chi-square = 11.843	df=6	Not Significant at 5 per cent level		
Occupational background				
Service	2 (11.1)	2 (11.1)	14 (77.8)	-
Business	34 (25.4)	46 (34.3)	40 (29.9)	14 (10.4)
Agriculture	2 (25.0)	4 (50.0)	2 (25.0)	-
Chi-square = 18.161	df=6	Significant at 5 per cent level		

Table-2.1 reveals that 56 per cent of the sample entrepreneurs were facing the problem of technological changes. Age-wise information further shows that this problem was faced by entrepreneurs of all the age groups. More than 56 per cent of entrepreneurs in all the age groups, except first and the last, were facing this problem. On the other hand, only 38 per cent of the entrepreneurs in the age group of less than 35 years were facing this problem. It shows that entrepreneurs in the lower age groups were more concerned with technological aspects of the business; moreover, for the new generation of entrepreneurs bringing about technological changes is much easier. The value of chi- square is statistically significant at 5 per cent level of significance. The hypothesis of no significant association between these two variables stands rejected.

Education-wise information further reveals that more than 50 per cent of the entrepreneurs having different levels of education had faced the problem of technological changes. This problem was felt even more by entrepreneurs possessing higher levels of education: It appeared that they were more concerned with the technological aspect and understanding its impact on the business. The value of chi-square is statistically insignificant. The hypothesis of no significant association between these two variables stands accepted.

The occupational background of entrepreneurs shows that the problem of technological changes was felt more by entrepreneurs coming from business families as compared to other entrepreneurs. It shows that entrepreneurs coming from business family background were aware of technological aspects of business and the complexities of business world, and required technological innovations more frequently. The value of chi-square is statistically significant, and hence the hypothesis of no significant association between these two variables stands rejected.

Table-2.2 shows the problems faced by the respondents while taking financial assistance from the financial institutions. Whereas taking loans from financial institutions was not a problem, 20 per cent of the entrepreneurs had reported problem in getting finance. There was a significant change in the perception of financial institutions while giving loans to small scale sector. The age-wise information shows that entrepreneurs in the middle age groups faced this problem more as compared to other entrepreneurs. The value of chi-square is statistically significant.

Education-wise, even the entrepreneurs possessing higher levels of education had faced problems in getting loan from financial institutions. Apparently, there was some gap in the process of taking loans. Only a small proportion of entrepreneurs (10%) having no formal level of education had faced the problem in getting the institutional loans. Of the graduate entrepreneurs, 24 per cent had agreed that taking loans from financial institutions was a problem. The value of chi-square is statistically significant. Therefore the hypothesis of no significant association between these two variable stands rejected.

Table - 2.2 : Problems of taking loans from financial institutions

Group	*To a great extent*	*To a large extent*	*To some extent*	*To little extent*	*Not at all*
All data	4 (2.5)	28 (17.5)	60 (37.5)	56 (35.0)	12 (7.5)
Age (years)					
Less than 35	2 (7.7)	2 (7.7)	12 (46.2)	10 (38.5)	-
35 to 40	-	2 (6.3)	20 (62.5)	6 (18.8)	4 (12.5)
40-45	2 (4.8)	8 (19.0)	16 (38.1)	14 (33.3)	2 (4.8)
45-50	-	12 (54.5)	2 (9.1)	6 (27.3)	2 (9.1)
Chi-square = 50.194 df = 16 Significant at 5 per cent level					
Education					
Schooling	-	6 (10.0)	22 (36.7)	28 (46.7)	4 (6.7)
Graduate	4 (5.4)	14 (18.9)	26 (35.1)	22 (29.7)	8 (10.8)
Post-graduate	-	8 (30.8)	12 (46.2)	6 (23.1)	-
Chi-square = 16.983 df = 8 Significant at 5 per cent level					
Occupational background					
Service	-	4 (22.2)	8 (44.4)	6 (33.3)	-
Business	4 (3.0)	22 (16.4)	50 (37.3)	48 (35.8)	-
Agriculture	-	2 (25.0)	2 (25.00)	2 (25.0)	2 (25.0)
Chi-square = 6.803 df = 8 Not Significant at 5 per cent level					

Table-2.3: Problems relating to transportation

Group	*To a great extent*	*To a large extent*	*To some extent*	*To little extent*	*Notat all*
All data	6 (3.8)	62 (38.8)	76 (47.5)	12 (7.5)	4 (2.5)
Age (years)					
Less than 35	-	12 (46.2)	10 (38.5)	4 (15.4)	-
35 to 40	2 (6.3)	14 (43.8)	14 (43.8)	2 (6.3)	-
40-45	2 (4.8)	16 (38.1)	18 (42.9)	4 (9.5)	2 (4.8)
45-50	-	12 (54.5)	8 (36.4)	-	2 (9.1)
50+	2 (5.3)	8 (21.1)	26 (68.4)	2 (5.3)	-
Chi-square = 23.992 df = 16 Not significant at 5 per cent level					

(Contd...)

Education					
Schooling	4 (6.7)	16 (26.7)	30 (50.0)	6 (10.0)	4 (6.2)
Graduate	-	34 (45.8)	34 (45.9)	6 (8.1)	-
Post-graduate	2 (7.7)	12 (46.2)	12 (46.2)	-	-
Chi-square = 18.110	df = 8	Significant at 5 per cent level			
Occupational background					
Service	4 (22.2)	4 (22.2)	8 (44.4)	2 (11.1)	-
Business	2 (1.5)	56 (41.8)	62 (46.3)	10 (7.5)	4 (3.0)
Agriculture	-	2 (25.0)	6 (75.0)	-	-
Chi-square = 23.520	df = 8	Significant at 5 per cent level			

backgrounds had faced this problem, while slightly more than one-fourth of the entrepreneurs coming from business families had faced this problem. The value of chi- square is statistically insignificant. The hypothesis of no significant association between these two variables stands accepted.

Table-2.3 highlights the problem of transportation faced by the sample entrepreneurs: 42 per cent of them had agreed that transportation of products was a problem for them. It shows that the small scale entrepreneurs were facing the problem of high cost of transportation; hence they had to sell their products in the local markets and, as a result, had to suffer losses.

The age-wise information shows that more than 42 per cent of the entrepreneurs in the age group of up to 50 years were facing transportation problem. Only a small proportion of entrepreneurs in the higher age groups had not complained of this problem. It reveals that entrepreneurs in this category might have established strong links in the nearby markets and were therefore not much affected by this factor. The new generation of entrepreneurs, however, found it a problem to compete with established entrepreneurs in the local markets. The value of chi square is statistically insignificant. Hence the hypothesis of no significant association between these two variables stands accepted.

The education-wise information shows that more than 45 per cent of the entrepreneurs possessing higher levels of education were facing the problem of transportation. It shows that even the educated entrepreneurs had failed to find a solution to this problem. The value of chi square is statistically significant. Therefore the hypothesis of no significant association between these two variables stands rejected. There is a need to further strengthen the infrastructure in order to reduce the cost of production.

The occupational background of the respondents reveals that entrepreneurs hailing from business families (58) were facing the problem of transportation more acutely than entrepreneurs coming from agriculture families (2). The analysis of data reveals that the intensity of the problem varied considerably among the entrepreneurs from business families. There is a need to provide some alternatives like facilities of railway and some other form of subsidies in order to reduce the problem of transportation faced by the small scale entrepreneurs so as to help them to sell their products in markets which fetch better price and ultimately more profit. The value of chi square is statistically significant. Thus the hypothesis of no significant association between these two variables stands rejected.

Table - 2.4: Problems relating to frequent power breakdown

Group	*To a great extent*	*To a large extent*	*To some extent*
All data	96 (60.0)	34 (28.3)	30 (18.8)
Age (years)			
Less than 35	22 (84.6)	2 (7.7)	2 (7.7)
35 to 40	24 (75.01)	4 (12.5)	4 (12.5)
40-45	24 (57.1)	10 (23.8)	8 (19.0)
45-50	8 (36.4)	8 (36.4)	6 (27.3)
50+	18 (47.4)	10 (26.3)	10 (26.3)
Chi-square = 17.673 df = 8 Significant at 5 per cent level			
Education			
Schooling	32 (53.3)	16 (26.7)	12 (20.0)
Graduate	46 (62.2	12 (16.2)	16 (21.6)
Post-graduate	18 (69.2)	6 (23.1)	2 (7.7)
Chi-square = 4.694 df = 4 Insignificant			
Occupational background			
Service	6 (33.3)	6 (33.3)	6 (33.3)
Business	88 (65.7)	24 (17.9)	22 (16.4)
Agriculture	2 (25.0)	4 (50.0)	2 (25.0)
Chi-square = 12.134 df = 4 Significant at 5 per cent level			

Table-2.4 projects the problem of frequent power breakdown faced by the respondent entrepreneurs. The majority of 88 per cent had agreed that they were facing the problem of frequent breakdown of power in their units. It shows that the problem was more intense and the small scale entrepreneurs did not have the capacity to install their own power generation sets to facilitate the smooth running of their production units like their large scale counterparts. As such they had to depend upon the State Electricity Boards for the regular power supply.

The age-wise information further projects that more than 75 per cent of the entrepreneurs in different age groups were facing the problem of frequent power break-down in their units. Over 90 entrepreneurs in the lower age groups were facing this problem. The value of chi square is statistically significant, and thus the hypothesis of no significant association between these two variables stands rejected.

As per the education-wise information, more than 75 per cent of the entrepreneurs having different levels of education were facing the problem of frequent power break- down in their units. It shows the intensity of their problem. The value of chi square is statistically insignificant. Therefore the hypothesis of no significant association between these two variables stands accepted.

The occupation-wise analysis shows that the problem of frequent power break-down was felt more by the entrepreneurs with business background (112) than those from service and agriculture families. The value of chi square is statistically significant, and thus the hypothesis of no significant association between these two variables stands rejected. There is a need to tackle energy problem on a priority basis because it is one of the main inputs for the industrial sector.

Table-2.5 highlights that more than 41 per cent of the sample entrepreneurs had agreed that getting information regarding various aspects of business was not easy for the small scale entrepreneurs. There is a need to enhance the availability of information to the small scale entrepreneurs.

The age-wise information reveals that entrepreneurs in the lower age groups were facing this problem more as compared to entrepreneurs in the higher age groups. More than 45 per cent of the entrepreneurs in age groups of up to 40 years had reported this problem, as against slightly less than 35 per cent of the entrepreneurs in the age group of beyond 45 years. The value of chi-square is statistically significant, and hence the hypothesis of no significant association between these two variables stands rejected.

More than 76 per cent of the entrepreneurs possessing higher levels of education had indicated difficulties in getting information relating to various problems. On the other hand, 40 per cent of the entrepreneurs with lower levels of education had complained of this problem. The analysis reveals that entrepreneurs having lower levels of education need more information and in this process may face the problem. There is a need to increase the level of awareness regarding the availability of information among the entrepreneurs through interaction between industry and government agencies. The value of chi-square is this problem. The value of chi-square is statistically significant, and the hypothesis of no significant association between these two variables stands rejected.

Table - 2.5: Problem of getting information

Group	*To a great extent*	*To a large extent*	*To some extent*	*To little extent*	*Not at all*
All data	8 (8.8)	62 (32.5)	36 (43.8)	50 (13.8)	4 (1.3)
Age (years)					
Less than 35	-	12 (46.2)	8 (30.8)	4 (15.4)	2 (7.7)
35 to 40	2 (6.3)	16 (50.0)	6 (18.8)	8 (25.0)	-
40-45	-	20 (47.6)	6 (14.3)	14 (33.3)	2 (4.8)
45-50	4 (18.2)	6 (27.3)	2 (9.1)	10 (45.5)	-
50+	2 (5.3)	8 (21.1)	14 (36.8)	14 (36.8)	-
Chi-square = 35.044	df = 16	Significant at 5 per cent level			
Education					
Schooling	4 (6.7)	20 (33.3)	12 (20.0)	24 (21.0)	-
Graduate Post-	4 (5.4)	22 (29.7)	22 (29.7)	24 (32.4)	2 (7.7)
graduate	-	20 (76.9)	2 (7.7)	2 (7.7)	2 (7.7)
Chi-square = 28.229	df = 8	Significant at10 per centlevel			
Occupational background					
Service	4 (22.2)	2 (11.1)	2 (11.1)	10 (55.6)	-
Business	4 (3.0)	60 (44.8)	32 (23.9)	34 (25.4)	4 (3.0)
Agriculture	-	-	2 (75.0)	6 (75.0)	-
Chi-square = 31.803	df = 8	Significant at10per cent level			

Conclusions

The foregoing analysis reveals that entrepreneurs in small scale sector face various infrastructural problems. Therefore the infrastructure for small scale sector needs to be further strengthened. The transportation system should be made cost-effective for small scale sector. Information needed by the small scale sector should be provided easily through various agencies and industrial associations. There should be frequent interaction between the government agencies and the associations of small scale enterprises. Awareness regarding the availability of information should be increased among the entrepreneurs. Technological aspects of small scale sector need to be taken into consideration by the institutes involved in technological development. Technological transformation should be made simple for small scale sector. Alternative sources of energy may be developed for small scale sector in particular and industry in general in order to make it more efficient in the emerging free markets.

3

Potential Technopreneurs and their Risk Taking Styles

– Regalla Ravi Kanth
M.S. Bhat
D. Raghunatha Reddy

Abstract

Risk taking has been reported consistently throughout entrepreneurship literature as an essential characteristic of entrepreneurs, and is well documented. However, there are various styles of risk taking as well as various measures of risk taking styles. Of particular interest, and perhaps the most employed measure, is ring toss, with the objective of measuring the risk taking styles among entrepreneurs. The present research has explored the potential of technoprenurs' risking style in a sample of 156 - 90 male and 66 female - B.Tech/ M.Tech graduates who were undergoing entrepreneurial development training for two weeks in Osmania University entrepreneurship development cell. The data was collected from the same centre and on a homogeneous sample but undergoing the entrepreneurship development training programmes at different times and in different batches. All of them were well versed with English and had more or less the same level of comprehension vis-a-vis the English language. The results are reported here after applying the appropriate statistics.

Key words: *Entrepreneur, ring toss, risk, risk taking styles, small and medium enterprises technopreneur.*

Introduction to entrepreneurship

Around the globe it is now conceded that entrepreneurship is necessary and immensely important for economic growth and well being. Further it is acknowledged as an effective instrument for fighting unemployment and poverty. To promote entrepreneurship, various efforts are made in the form of training programmes with the belief that entrepreneurs are not born but made.

Around 1940, development of entrepreneurs began to be targeted through various policies such as grants, credits at lower rate and tax holidays, which were used as special incentives for small businesses and small and medium entrepreneurs. It was realised as early as in 1948 in Japan; the above mentioned facts are supported by observations of Glaub, & Frese, 2011 (www.oecd.org/cfe/smes/31919278.pdf).

It is now recogonised universally and admitted by scholars that entrepreneurship is fundamental to economy and is also a catalyst for innovation, providing new jobs and taking the economy to the next higher level. Evidence for these observations comes from Baumol (2002); Birch (1987); van Stel (2006).

An enduring observation amongst scholars reveals with the notion that entrepreneurship is of fundamental importance for the economy as it functions as a catalyst for innovation, job creation and economic well being. Scientific evidence for this relationship has accumulated over time. Developing countries accept that entrepreneurship with its inherent economic potential becomes a very effective tool in eradicating poverty and generating employment. Therefore promotion of entrepreneurship is used as an approach in most of the developing countries (Mead & Liedholm 1998; Martinez et al. 2010).

Thus it is seen that government and their policy makers have looked at entrepreneurship training programme for generating income, creating jobs, and maximum utilisation of local resourses, which they believe will promote a balanced development of different regions.

The National Science and Technology Entrepreneurship Development Board (NSTEDB) established in 1982 by the Government of India under the Department of Science and Technology, aims to percolate entrepreneurship to the level of the most under-privileged, depressed groups such as Scheduled Castes and Scheduled Tribes (Department of Science and Technology, Annual Report 2013-14).

The current prime minister of our country often says, 'We are job makers, not job takers'(Indian express.com November 13, 2015 New Delhi).

Risk and entrepreneurship

As early as the recorded history and perhaps even earlier, individuals were taking risk in various activities: for example, hunting animals for food. This view is vetted by Grier (1980, 1981). An entrepreneur is one who conceives, organises and frequently undertakes risks. Almost all (100%) entrepreneurs have listed risk as the most preferred characteristic and have ranked it as the most preferred characteristic- precisely 98 per cent as reported by Vivek Wadhawa et.al (Wadhwa et al. 2009).

Richard Cantilon (1755), who is known as father of entrepreneurship, in his essay on economic theory, has characterised the entrepreneur as risk bearer. Frank Knight (1921) identifies risk-taking ability as the most integral element in defining entrepreneurial characteristics. Risk runs as a key element in entrepreneur literature (e.g., Ahmed 1985; Caliendo, Fossen, & Kritikos 2010; Koh 1996; Long 1983).

Olson (1986), for example, declares that the ability of risk taking is gainful in generating new business, while Cromie (2000) suggests that the talent and willingness to tolerate and overcome risk are quite essential when engaging in entrepreneurial activity. Recent research by Caliendo, Fossen, and Kritikos (2010) finds that risk attitudes can prolong the patience of an entrepreneur. And Fairlie and Holleran (2012) establish proof to suggest that risk tolerance predisposes small entrepreneurs to benefit more from entrepreneurship training.

The common feeling is that the entrepreneur has unusual appetite for risk; however, this belief has received mixed support. Stewart and Roth's twenty years of meta-analysis of research on general risk-taking attitudes of entrepreneurs found that entrepreneurs possess a higher risk propensity than their counterparts called managers (2001). Miner and Raju (2004), in their meta-analysis studies using measures of risk-taking motives (as opposed to attitudes), find that entrepreneurs are generally risk-avoiding. Further Miner and Raju feel that it is far too early to draw conclusions about the relationship between entrepreneurship and individual differences with respect to risk taking abilities of individuals.

According to happy schools.com, more than 60 per cent of the Indian population possesses personality traits that are critical for success as entrepreneur — business thinking (69%), optimism (66%), and persistence (65%) — which proposes a wealth of entrepreneurial capacity. However, readiness to take the risk of running a business is not a general character of majority of Indians (http://www.happyschools.com /indians-are-not-risk-takers).

Methodology

Sample

For the present research study 156 promising entrepreneurs-90 male and 66 female together-who finished B.Tech/ M.Tech were selected as sample. The sample was drawn from various entrepreneurship development programmes which were exclusively conducted at EDC Osmania University Hyderabad, for science and technology graduates. The youngest participant in these programmes was aged 23 years and the oldest was 37 years, while the average age of the sample was 25 years. This experience reveals that most of the young engineering graduates undergo entrepreneurship training in order to become entrepreneurs.

Operational definitions

In the present research the following operational definitions have been adopted by the authors.

MICRO SMALL AND MEDIUM ENTERPRISES: The Government of India (GoI), has passed the Micro, Small and Medium Enterprises Development (MSMED) Act, 2006 which came to be enforced from on 2nd October 2006 onwards. With the enactment of MSMED Act 2006, the standard shift that has taken place is the inclusion of the services sector in the definition of MSMEs, apart from extending the scope to medium enterprises. Thus, the MSMEDAct, 2006 has adapted the definition of micro, small and medium enterprises to units engaged in manufacturing or production as well as those providing or rendering services. The Reserve Bank has informed the changes to all scheduled commercial banks. Further, the definition, as per the Act, has been adopted for the purpose of bank credit vide RBI circular ref. RPCD. PLNFS.BC. No. 63/06.02.31/2006-07 Dated April 4, 2007 (https://rbi.org.in//BS_VscriptsiewMasCircular details.aspx?id=9018).

TECHNOPRENEURS: The present sample is comprised of those who have studied B.E. /B.Tech or M.E/ M.Tech and who wish to start an enterprise using their technical knowledge. Hence, they are called potential technopreneurs in the present research study.

Risk measurement:Risk could be measured by different instruments used by various authors, but present researchers adopted 'ring toss', a behavioural simulation exercise which is used by David McCleland. This exercise, first used by Kurt Lewin, is effectively used to study the risk taking behaviour by Venkatasubramanyam et al. (2009). In general, all over the world simulation exercises have been highlighted by David McCleland in the context of entrepreneurial development training to identify entrepreneurial talents.

Ring toss simulation

Instructions

The ring toss simulation exercise is process oriented and structurally very strong, for the simulation exercise instructions play a very important role. All the participants are made to sit properly after the preliminary registration process and the organisers commenced session-I, i.e., entrepreneurial motivation training, after a brief introduction about entrepreneurship. It is important to the participants that the following instructions were imparted after showing the rings and the wooden peg. These rings are12 inches in diameter, made up of cane, and the task involves tossing the ring and throwing it on to the peg. Hence this exercise is called 'ring toss'. "The distance is measured in feet, starting from peg one. Up to 10 feet distance is marked, irrespective of the distance. If the ring falls on the peg neatly it fetches three points; if it hits the peg without falling in it two points; and in other cases no points are earned. Once the distance is chosen by the participant, three rings are given to each participant. All the rings are thrown from the same distance for the chosen round. All the participants' rounds are cleared". The second and third rounds are not declared at the time of first round instructions. All the scores are recorded in a tabular form on a sheet and discussed. The prize money is given to the winner.

ROUND ONE(SOLO ROUND): Round one is called solo/ individual round. Only the person will come and throw the ring in the presence of trainer.

ROUND TWO (GROUP/SOCIAL ROUND): Round two is called group round because in this round along with the participant thrower, the fellow throwers /participants are also present.

ROUND THREE (GROUP/SOCIAL PLUS MONEY): In round three, along with all participants prize money is also introduced. Hence it is called socio economic round.

Rationale of ring toss

The distance chosen by participants reveals the risk taken by the participant, one foot to four feet distance from the peg is defined as lower risk taker, five to six feet is moderate risk taker, and seven feet and the distance beyond is called high risk taker.

Statistics and analysis

Using spss 16.0 independent t-value was calculated. Based on the analysis the following null hypotheses were formulated, analysed and interpreted.

H0: In the individual round, there is no difference in male and female techno entrepreneurs'risk taking styles.

The statistics pertaining to round 1 are tabulated and presented in tables 3.1a and 3.1b as follows.

Table - 3.1a: Group statistics: individual risk

Gender	*N*	*Mean*	*Std. deviation*	*Std. error mean*
Male	90	2.5222	.64001	.06746
Female	66	2.1364	.55154	.06789

Table -3.1b: Independent samples test

	Levene's test for equality of variances		*T-test for equality of means*						
	F	*Sig.*	*T*	*Df*	*Sig. (2-tailed)*	*Mean Difference*	*Std. error difference*	*95% Confidence interval of the difference*	
								Lower	*Upper*
Equal variances assumed	11.632	.001	3.940	154	.000	.38586	.09792	.19241	.57930
Equal variances not assumed			4.032	149.999	.000	.38586	.09571	.19675	.57497

An independent sample t-test was conducted to compare male and female risk taking styles in the individual round. There was significant difference between the male (M= 2.52, SD= .64) and female risk taking score (M=2.13, SD = .55) conditions; t (154) = 3.94, p=0.00. These results suggest that the potential male and female entrepreneurs have significant difference in risk taking styles. Specifically, these results suggest that when potential male and female engineering graduates and post- graduates become entrepreneurs, promising male entrepreneurs are more risk prone than their female counterparts.

H0: In the group round, there is no difference in male and female techno entrepreneurs'risk taking styles.

The statistics pertaining to round-2 are tabulated and shown in tables 3.2a and 3.2b as given below.

Table - 3.2a: Group statistics: risk in the presence of fellow trainees

Gender	*N*	*Mean*	*Std. deviation*	*Std. error mean*
Male	90	2.2778	.68741	.07246
Female	66	1.6970	.63172	.07776

Table - 3.2b: Independent samples test

	Levene's test for equality of variances		*T-test for equality of means*						
	F	*Sig.*	*T*	*Df*	*Sig. (2-tailed)*	*Mean difference*	*Std. error difference*	*95% Confidence interval of the difference*	
								Lower	*Upper*
Equal variances assumed	.716	.399	5.394	154	.000	.58081	.10768	.36808	.79353
Equal variances not assumed			5.465	146.319	.000	.58081	.10629	.37075	.79086

An independent sample t-test was conducted to compare male and female risk taking styles in the social round. There was significant difference in the male risk taking scores (M= 2.27, SD= .68) and female risk taking scores (M=1,69, SD = .63) conditions; t (154) = 5.39, p=0.00. These results suggest that in the group round, i.e., in the presence of other fellow trainees, male and female potential entrepreneurs have significant difference in risk taking styles. Specifically these results suggest that when male and female engineering graduates and post-graduates become entrepreneurs, male promising entrepreneurs are more risk prone than their female counterparts.

H0: In the socio economic round, there is no difference in male and female techno entrepreneurs'risk taking styles.

Table - 3.3a: Group statistics: socio economic round

Gender	*N*	*Mean*	*Std. deviation*	*Std. error mean*
Male	90	2.1333	.63952	.06741
Female	66	1.5909	.55407	.06820

Table - 3.3b: Independent samples test

	Levene's test for equality of variances		*T-test for equality of means*						
	F	*Sig.*	*T*	*Df*	*Sig. (2-tailed)*	*Mean difference*	*Std. error difference*	*95% Confidence interval of the difference*	
								Lower	*Upper*
Equal variances assumed	.474	.492	5.533	154	.000	.54242	.09803	.34876	.73609
Equal variances not assumed			5.656	149.696	.000	.54242	.09589	.35294	.73191

An independent sample t-test was conducted to compare male and female risk taking styles in the presence of group members including money. Hence this round was called as socio-economic round. There was a significant difference in the male (M= 2.13, SD= .69) and female risk taking scores (M=1.59, SD = .55) conditions; t (154) = 5.53, p=0.00. These results suggest that the potential male and female entrepreneurs have significant difference in the socio-economic round also. Specifically these results suggest that when male and female engineering graduates and post- graduates become entrepreneurs, male promising entrepreneurs are more risk prone than their female counterparts.

Conclusion

From the three rounds of ring toss experiment,with a sample size of 166 participants, (both male and female), it is evident that potential male technopreneurs have higher propensity for taking risks than their female counterparts.

4

IDENTIFYING POSSIBLE ENTREPRENEURS: AN INDIAN STUDY

– *VIVEK SHARMA*
SUDHIR K. JAIN

Abstract

Promotion of entrepreneurship is the most coveted aim of Indian policy makers in present times. Rising population on the one hand and lack of employment opportunities on the other point to the need for entrepreneurship promotion. However, this is easier said than done. Introduction of simultaneous LPG reforms is known to have led to increased interaction of political and economic roles performed by government functionaries which, in turn, led to an unholy alliance of self-interest and lack of established systems in post-socialist market economies. As these societies embrace 'self-interest' to be a legitimate motive of action, they are generally devoid of established systems to keep the processes under check, thereby lending unbridled powers to government employees. This makes government sector employment to be the most preferred option in such societies and entrepreneurship naturally takes a back seat. India adopted LPG reforms in 1991 and is one such economy in many aspects, where entrepreneurship orientation among graduates is a rare phenomenon. Using data on 564 graduating students of professional courses in the Jammu & Kashmir State of India, the paper proposes a discriminant model, based on indigenously developed factors and demographics, in order to identify the youngsters who are likely to take up entrepreneurship as an employment option, so that the efforts of entrepreneurship promotion can be logically directed, instead of wasteful promotion by way of subsidy schemes.

Keywords: *Discriminant model, entrepreneurship promotion, entrepreneurship orientation, Jammu & Kashmir, LPG reforms, post-socialist market economies*

Introduction

Economic development and entrepreneurial activity have been repeatedly reinforced as effect and cause by researches carried out over

time (Toma et al. 2014; Szirmai et al. 2011; Naude 2011; Pfeifer & Sarlia 2010; Carree and Thurik 2010; Walzer 2009; Audretsch et al. 2006). Koster and Rai (2008) went a step ahead when they suggested that developmental policy should mainly aim at fostering entrepreneurship. Significantly, literature has also elucidated that entrepreneurship is dependent on the society's structural, political and cultural features (Begley et al. 2005; Berglund 2015; Hindle, 2010; Meek et al. 2010; Trettin & Welter 2011; Huggins and William 2011; Zeffane 2014). Post-socialist market economies have displayed a unique relationship between self-interest and lack of established systems (Bandelj 2016), thereby resulting in an over-preference for government sector employment (Sharma 2017).
in an over-preference for government sector employment (Sharma 2017).
India adopted the reforms of Liberalisation, Privatisation and Globalisation (LPG) rather recently. This classifies India as a post- socialist market economy. There is a huge need to create and refine a process of identifying students who are likely to undertake self-employment, based on indigenously developed factors, applicable to Indian context. The present paper attempts to use the factors affecting employment preferences, as reported by Sharma (2017), in order to generate significant inputs for understanding the entrepreneurial intentions among the youth of Indian society.

Development policies in post-socialist market economies

Literature has been increasingly pointing out the peculiarities of the developmental patterns in such economies. The new found orientations of a market economy seem to justify greed and self-interest as legitimate motives for action in an economy where lack of established systems leads to informality in the modus- operandi (Bandelj 2016). Many a researcher undertaking research on macro- developmental patterns has been resorting to the tools of economic sociology in the recent times (Schrank 2015). It is being increasingly theorised that the socio- economic systems act as embedded economies (Krippner and Alvarez 2007; Bandelj and Sowers 2010) and govern the behaviour of individuals. In the case of transitional economies making a shift from socialist development patterns to LPG regimes, this shift from socialism to capitalism is known to encourage what is called political capitalism (Staniszkis 1991), where the politicians, entrusted with the developmental as well as the welfare roles, tend to make use of their informational advantage towards generating personal benefits. Rapid privatisation under LPG reforms brings about information asymmetries and is generally coupled with lack of effective governance systems (Stiglitz 2000). Such an environment has been seen to foster corruption because of multiple opportunities available to do so, in wake of his work as a politician. Further, there are opportunities for rent-seeking and asset-stripping as well, in the absence of established systems preventing those. These informational asymmetries lead to concentration of power and knowledge in the hands of those who work in government jobs and thereby make it the most coveted employment option, making entrepreneurship promotion a much difficult task.

Research imperative

Most of the states in post-socialistic market economies display an ever increasing affinity towards government jobs and unless the entrepreneurs are simultaneously identified, assisted and idolised, a positive social and economic change towards entrepreneurship is unlikely, notwithstanding the subsidies and tax sops handed as bait by the policy makers. But identification of potential entrepreneurs at career starting age is a difficult challenge. Although research has accepted intentions as the most viable precursor to action, most of the intention based models have evolved in the western societies. As such there is a strong need for an indigenously developed model to identify potential entrepreneurs in Indian society.

Research objective

Based on data drawn from one such society viz. the state of Jammu & Kashmir, the present paper attempts to create a discriminant model in order to identify youngsters possessing Entrepreneurial Intentions (EI) at the career starting age. The study is built on indigenously identified factors affecting employment preferences of Government Sector Employment (GSE), Private Sector Employment (PSE) and Self-Employment (SE).

Research methodology

The population considered for the study was the graduating youth who were at the border stage between education and employment. At this stage of their education, they are most likely to have done a reality check about their vocational choice in general (Urbanaviciute et al. 2016). A sample of 564 respondents was considered for the study, well in excess of the required number of 398 based on the formula by Yamane (1967).

The respondents were subjected to four questions, as follows.

S1: Do you have any business idea that you would want to launch?

S2: Are you looking to design a product that can solve current problems?

S3: Do you intend to start own enterprise with a new business idea?

S4: Do you have an idea to create a product that can fulfill customer's unmet needs?

The respondents who answered affirmatively (210, 52.5%) to the question, S1 or S2, were taken to possess EI and those who marked all the four statements in negative were taken to be devoid of EI (190, 47.5%). All the others, viz. those who had marked yes to either S3 or S4 were not considered for the discriminant analysis as they belonged to a category that seemed to have a positive disposition towards entrepreneurship but its manifestation was not likely to be immediate and as such they were not likely to have given closer thought to the entrepreneurship decision and problems therein.

This differentiation, thus taken to be the response variable Y, was binary in nature with two levels. The independent variables considered in the analysis were categorical or nominal (table-4.1).

$$Y_i = \begin{cases} \dfrac{1;\text{Not possessing EI}}{2;\text{Possessing EI}} \end{cases}$$

Application and results of discriminant analysis

Discriminant analysis (DA) has been applied to determine the variables which could effectively contribute to distinguishing the individuals possessing EI from those not possessing it (Hair et al. 2010). Discriminant analysis requires the dependent variable to be categorical as represented by Yi. The independent variables are categorical in case of demographic variables and metric in case of factor variables. Using IBM SPSS Statistics 20, a discriminant function was derived, which separated the two groups (e.g., those having EI and those not having EI). Results were then assessed for predictive accuracy by developing a classification matrix (Hair et al. 2010). Using the above method, a series of discriminant functions was generated based on linear combinations of the predictor variables. For each new observation, the discriminant scores were obtained by using the discriminant function. The discriminant function is represented by the equation:

$$Y_i = C + B_1X_1 + B_2X_2 + \ldots\ldots B_nX_n$$

where Yi is the dependent categorical variable, C is the constant, B_1, B_2, B_3... B_n are the calculated coefficients of various variables and X_1, X_2 X_n are the variable values of the subjects to be calculated. The discriminant equation was generated based on the value of constant as well as the coefficients generated by the analysis.

To determine the impact of various variables on the intention to involve in entrepreneurship, discriminant analysis technique has been used (Hair et al. 2010). The present study adopted the enter step-wise method to estimate the discriminant functions. To determine the discriminant functions the results have been segregated into different sub-sections.

Table - 4.1: Dependent and independent variables considered for identifying entrepreneurs

Target Variable	*Notation*	*Description*
Entrepreneurial intention	Y	1 = Not possessing EI; 2 = Possessing EI
Demographic variables		
Gender	x_1	0 = Male; 1 = Female
Home region	x_2	0 = Jammu; 1 = otherwise
Academic performance	x_3	0 = 65 % or below; 1 = greater than 65%
Father's education	x_4	0 = Under-graduate; 1 = Graduate and above
Business background	x_5	0 = At least one parent in Business/SE; 1 = No parent in SE
Monthly family income	x_6	0 = up to ₹ 25000 p.m.; 1 = greater than ₹ 25000 p.m.
Factor variables		
Reasons for starting own business	x_7	Table 8
Social perception of entrepreneurship	x_8	Table 8
Advantage of own business	x_9	Table 8
Ease of doing business	x_{10}	Table 8
Attractiveness of GSE	x_{11}	Table 9
Politician-Govt. employee nexus	x_{12}	Table 9
Ease of GSE	x_{13}	Table 9
Disadvantages of PSE	x_{14}	Table 10
Stay-back tendency	x_{15}	Table 11
Ease of finding merit-based job under Protective environment of J&K	x_{16}	Table 11
Perceptions of compromise borne out of exclusivity	x_{17}	Table 11

The basic relationship between the variable used has been identified with the help of Karl Pearson correlation coefficient. The level of correlation pertaining to the factors used in the discriminant analysis was determined and the results pertaining to the test for assumption of multi-collinearity presented below. This is followed by the results about the equality of means for each variable used in the final analysis on the basis of Wilks' Lambda and the discussion associated with the procedure of the model, including the discussion about the assumption of homoscedasticity, and elaboration of the functions at group centriods and cut-off scores from the overall perspective, in the context of discriminant functions.

Finally, measurements of predictive validity and validation of the results obtained through the discriminant analysis are discussed (Hair et al. 2010).

Independent variables used for discriminant analysis

Table-4.1 presents the discussion pertaining to Karl Pearson's correlation coefficient, with respect to the variables adopted in the final model of discriminant analysis.

Table - 4.2: Correlation table to identify independent variables for DA

Independent variables	*Correlation with Y_i*
x_1	0.210*
x_2	0.078
x_3	-0.035
x_4	-0.039
x_5	0.183*
x_6	-0.056
x_7	0.114**
x_8	0.033
x_9	0.156*
x_{10}	0.141*
x_{11}	-0.024
x_{12}	0.032
x_{13}	-0.015
x_{14}	-0.007
x_{15}	0.044
x_{16}	0.129*
x_{17}	0.019

*Statistically significant at 1 % level of confidence.

**Statistically significant at 5 % level of confidence.

The results depict that the dependent variable Y (Entrepreneurial Intention) is having a statistically significant correlation with variables x1, x5, x7, x9, x10 and x16 (table-4.2). Further analysis involved investigation regarding the assumption of multi- collinearity among these variables.

Assumption of multi-collinearity

The correlations of the short-listed independent variables are reported in table-4.3. Variable x7 correlated significantly (on statistical grounds) with variables x9 and x10 and as such was removed. Also variable x10 correlated significantly (on statistical grounds) with variable x9 as well as variable x16. Thus variable x10 was also removed from the list of independent variables.

Table - 4.3: Correlation for significant independent variables

	x_1	x_5	x_7	x_9	$x10$	$x16$
x_1	1					
x_5	0.017	1				
x_7	0.018	0.030	1			
x_9	-0.012	0.186*	0.368*	1		
x10	0.107**	-0.039	0.342*	0.283**	1	
x16	-0.028	0.122**	-0.000	0.059	0.084**	1

*Statistically significant at 1 % level of significance
**Statistically significant at 5 % level of significance

The demographic variable x5 also correlated significantly with extracted factor variables x9 and x16 (table-4.4). Still, it was decided to include x5 in the final analysis because of it being a demographic variable unlike the other two which are extracted factor variables based on respondent's preferences and, moreover, the level of relationship is very low.

Table - 4.4: Correlation table for dependent variables finally used in DA

x_1	x_5	x9	x16	
x_1	1			
x_5	0.017	1		
x_9	-0.012	0.186*	1	
x16	-0.028	0.122**	0.059	1

*Statistically significant at 1 % level of significance
**Statistically significant at 5 % level of significance

Wilks'lambda & assumption of homoscedasticity

The DA has been conducted by entering all the four variables together. Table-4.5 presents the results of test for equality of group means for each variable on the basis of Wilks' lambda, also referred to as the U-statistic (Hair et al. 2010). The smaller the value of the lambda, the greater is the difference in the means of the two groups. In case of the four factors involved in this DA, all the differences were significant at 1 per cent level of significance. Therefore, group means as represented by Wilks' lambda were significantly different for all the four selected variables (table-4.5). However, Wilks' lambda provides little information about the effectiveness of the discriminant function in classification. It only provides a test of the null hypothesis that the population means are equal. The null hypotheses were rejected in case of all the four variables.

Moreover, the Box's M value was 11.450 with significance level of 0.333. Thus, null hypothesis of the population covariance matrices being equal was rejected and the assumption of homoscedasticity was nullified.

Results of discriminant analysis

To develop the model, discriminant loadings method has been used to determine the relative importance of each independent variable in discriminating the groups.

Table - 4.5: Results of discriminant analysis

							Classification functions	
Discriminant function	*Wilks' lambda*	*F-Ratio*	*Sig. level*	*Unstand-ardised*	*Standar-dised*	*Structure matrix*	*Group 1 Not having EI*	*Group 2 Having EI*
x1	0.956	18.315	.000	1.405	0.678	0.629	2.811	3.769
x5	0.967	13.723	.000	0.970	0.457	0.544	-0.827	-0.166
x9	0.976	9.968	.002	0.130	0.407	0.464	1.252	1.340
x16	0.983	6.727	.010	0.207	0.357	0.381	1.957	2.098
(Constant)	-	-	-	-4.109	-		-14.821	-17.509

The variables having loadings greater that 0.50 are considered very significant while variables having loadings greater that 0.40 but lesser than 0.50 are considered important and variables with loadings greater than or equal to 0.3 but lesser that 0.4 are considered significant (Hair et al. 2010). The structure matrix revealed that the loadings were above +0.3 in case of all the 4 variables. In view of all of the above, the proposed discriminant model seemed statistically viable. Variable x16 had structure matrix value greater than 0.3 but less than 0.4. Variable x9 had structure matrix value greater than 0.4 but less than 0.5 while x1 and x5 had structure matrix values greater than 0.5 (table-4.5).

Calculating cut-off scores using DA

This section reports the group means of the generated discriminant function. The value of group centroids is used to interpret discriminant function results from a holistic perspective. These are un-standardised canonical discriminant functions evaluated at group means and they indicate a most typical location of any individual from a particular group while the group centroids show as to how apart they are along the dimensions selected. As depicted in table-4.6, the group centroid for group-1 (Not having EI is -0.358 and the centroid for group-2 (Having EI) is 0.324. The group centroids are interpreted as the number of standard deviations that each group is away from the average of both groups taken together (Hair et al. 2010). With standardised data, the average of all the groups becomes zero. This can be checked by multiplying the frequency of each group with its centroid $\{210 \times 0.324 + 190 \times (-0.358) = 0\}$. On the average, respondents not having EI have a larger discriminant function than those who have EI.

Table - 4.6: Group means (centroids) of evolved discriminant function

1- Not having EI 2- Having EI	*Function*
1	-0.358
2	0.324

In the sample of 400 respondents possessing EI, the dependent variable consisted of two groups, 190 respondents not having EI and 210 respondents having EI. Since the sample was randomly drawn, it can be taken to reflect population proportions. Thus sample proportions were used to specify the prior probabilities for classification purposes (Hair et al. 2010). The optimum discriminant score was obtained by calculating weighted average of the two group centroids (see table-4.6 for centroid values):

$$Z_{CS} = \frac{NaZb \quad Za}{Na+Nb} = \frac{190 \times (0.324) + 210 \times (-0.358)}{190 + 210} = -0.03405$$

The cutting score of -0.03405 suggests that:

(i) A respondent shall be identified as being in group-1 (Not having EI) if its discriminant score is less than 0.03405.

(ii) Arespondent shall be identified as being in group-2 (Having EI) if its discriminant score is greater than 0.03405.

Predictive model accuracy

The predictive accuracy of the discriminant model is obtained from the classification matrix (table-4.7).

Table - 4.7: Predicted group membership

			Predicted group membership		
			1	*2*	*Total*
Observed	Count (%)	1	115 (60.5%)	75 (39.5%)	190
Group membership		2	67 (31.9%)	143 (68.1%)	210
Cross- validated	Count (%)	1	110 (57.9%)	80 (42.1%)	190
		2	72 (34.3%)	138 (65.7%)	210

Percentage of well classified respondents = 64.5

There are three methods of evaluating classification accuracy. The classification accuracy of the model was checked by using all the three.

Discussion on validation of the DAmodel

The evolved model for identifying entrepreneurs needs to be evaluated for predictive accuracy (Hair et al. 2010). This was done by using three different methods as discussed below.

Random chance criterion of evaluating predictive accuracy

The first method of measuring the predictive accuracy is the comparison with the chance accuracy. This method is used in case of equal group sizes. Chance accuracy is defined as the probability of a random case belonging to the maximum probability group. In this case, there is a higher probability of a random case belonging to group-2 as the chance of a random case belonging to group-2 (Having EI) is 52.5 per cent. But the predictive probability of the model is 64.5 per cent. For justification of the model the predictive probability must be at least 25 per cent better that the chance probability (Hair et al. 2010: 263). That sets a standard of 52.5 x 1.25 = 65.6 per cent. The predictive probability of our model is thus, quite close to the required standard.

Proportional Chance Criterion method of evaluating predictive accuracy

This method is used in case of unequal group sizes (Hair et al. 2010: 262). Although the groups are almost of equal sizes, the method has been applied as a cross- reference. The proportional chance criterion assumes that the costs of miscalculation are equal. The proportional chance criterion is $C_{PRO} = p^2 + (1 - p)^2$ where,

C_{PRO} =Proportional chance criterion &

p=Proportion of respondents in Group 1
1-p=Proportion of respondents in Group 2

In this case p = (190/400 = 0.475) and (1 - p) = (210/400 = 0.525). Therefore, C_{PRO} = 0.05.

The proportional chance criterion is 5 per cent. In order for the discriminant function to be of practical significance, its hit ratio should exceed the CPRO by 25 per cent (Hair et al. 2010). In other words it should be (5 x 1.25= 6.25%). The hit ratio of our model is 64.5 per cent (table-4.7) which is significantly higher than the desired level.

Statistics based measure (Press's Q) of classification accuracy

Press's Q statistic is used to compare the number of correct classifications with the total sample size and number of groups (Hair et al. 2010: 263). This calculated value is then compared with a critical value (chi-square value for 1 degree of freedom at the desired level of confidence). If the calculated value exceeds the critical value, the classification matrix can be deemed better than pure chance. The Q statistic is calculated by the following formula:

Press's Q = $[N - (nK)]^2 / N (K - 1)$

Where N = Total sample size

nK= Number of observations correctly classified

K = number of groups

In the present case, N = 400; n = 258 and K = 2.

Therefore, using the formula, Press's Q statistic is 50.41. The critical value at the significance level of 0.01 is 6.8. Thus, it can be concluded that in this case the predictions are significantly better than chance.

Thus, all the three methods of validation viz. Random chance criterion, Proportional chance criterion and Press's Q formula authenticate the classification matrix to be statistically better than chance alone. This indigenously developed model, developed in a post-socialistic market economy, is capable of identifying potential entrepreneurs among graduating students. After testing in other societies, it can be used by the government agencies to spot and nurture entrepreneurs and avoid wasteful practices of entrepreneurship promotion through subsidies/ protectionism.

Conclusion

As put by McKinsey estimates (Gupta et al. 2014), India's working-age population will grow by 690 lakh between 2012 and 2022. It would require a whooping 690 lakh additional jobs, if India is to encash on its demographic potential. This is in addition to the present jobs. Estimates indicate that to pursue an inclusive reforms agenda, India needs an additional 115 lakh non-farm jobs in the next decade. Creation of new businesses is therefore an important issue in the Indian context. The same report records that *Global Entrepreneurship Monitor* that tracks entrepreneurial activity found that new business ownership rate for India in 2013 was the same as in 2008. This indigenously developed model is capable of identifying potential entrepreneurs among graduating students within India. Since it is based on demographic and extracted factors based on the responses of graduating Indian students, this model is likely to be a better predictor of entrepreneurial intentions among graduating students than a non-indigenous model.

The expert committee recommendations report of NITI Aayog (2015:20) has explicitly recognised that Indian education system is grossly unprepared for innovation economy. It further says that World Bank has suggested that India is seen as a country facing skills shortage caused by a lack of skills development and an unresponsive education system. The identification of entrepreneurial intent and its culturing is thus a goal of paramount importance for educationists. The presented discriminant model can be applied by the college authorities in the beginning sessions of graduation so as to identify the students having entrepreneurial intentions. Later- on, special training can be imparted to these identified students so that entrepreneurship orientation can be strengthened and further sharpened. This shall go a long way in avoiding wasteful practices of entrepreneurship promotion through subsidies/protectionism.

Annexures

Table - 4.8: Factors affecting preference of self-employment/ business (Mean & Standard Deviations)

F -1	*Reasons for starting own business*	*Mean*	*S.D.*
S -1	Getting a regular govt. job in J&K is very difficult.	3.76	1.287
S -2	Getting a good private job in J&K is difficult.	3.72	1.355
S -3	Through own business, it is possible to create more wealth by putting more time & effort.	3.96	1.150

(Contd...)

S -4	In business one gets freedom to work according to own time schedule.	3.76	1.249
S -5	In own enterprise, one does not have to work under bosses.	3.96	1.236
F -2	***Social perception of entrepreneurship***		
S -6	My society encourages youngsters to become entrepreneurs.	1.96	1.032
S -7	My society does not encourage youngsters to becomeentrepreneurs.	2.04	1.090
F -3	***Advantages of own business***		
S -8	In business there is stability of place of stay.	3.05	1.223
S -9	In business support of other family members isgenerally available.	3.03	1.242
S -10	In business, living with parents is possible.	3.71	1.243
S -11	In business, parent support for bringing up children becomes easily available.	3.11	1.176
F -4	***Ease of doing business***		
S-12	Most businessmen/entrepreneurs form associations which deal with various govt. agencies and inspectors.	3.38	1.056
S-13	Business associations help in resolving issues associated with various govt. agencies and inspectors.	3.17	1.012
S-14	It is not difficult to start own business enterprise.	2.6 7	1.286

Source: Author.

(The factor values of the generated factors can be supplied on request.)

Table - 4.9: Factors affecting preference of GSE (Mean & Standard Deviations)

F-5	***Attractiveness of GSE***	***Mean***	***S.D.***
S-15	People prefer a government job because it involves higher prestige.	4.03	1.130
S-16	People prefer a government job because it involves power.	3.73	1.216
S-17	People in government job can easily get various jobs done, through networking.	3.51	1.232
S- 18	Government job is the most secure employment option.	3.98	1.275
S-19	People prefer a government job because of non-salary perks /benefits.	3.41	1.289
S-20	In government job, success is defined as "good" posting.	3.79	1.204
F-6	***Politician and government-employee nexus***		
S-21	In government job, success can be achieved through politicians' favours.	3.55	1.270
S-22	Politicians favour those employees who help them in generating money.	3.87	1.244
S-23	Politicians favour those government employees who execute their verdict & wishes.	3.83	1.252

(Contd...)

F-7	*Ease of GSE*		
S-24	People in government job have lesser work load than those in corporate sector.	3.89	1.260
S-25	People in government job have lesser work load than those in self-employment.	3.77	1.252

Source: Author.
(The factor values of the generated factors can be supplied on request.)

Table - 4.10: Factor loadings for factors of PSE

F-8	*Disadvantages of PSE*	*Mean*	*S.D.*
S-26	Corporate sector jobs do not provide job security.	2.33	1.268
S-27	Due to longer working hours in corporate jobs, one gets less time for own family.	2.06	1.199
S-28	Corporate jobs are more demanding in terms of performance.	2.14	1.139
S-29	Corporate jobs involve high stress and tension because of time bound target achievement expectations.	2.13	1.193

Source: Author.
(The factor values of the generated factors can be supplied on request.)

Table - 4.11: Factor loadings for factors affecting employment preferences

F-1	*Stay back tendency*	*Mean*
S-1	In business families with 2 or more sons the parents want one of them to take-up an administrative job in J&K.	3.29
S-2	I am determined to stay back in J&K for my career.	3.13
S-3	I would rather earn less income by working near to home than earn higher income away from home or outside J&K.	3.26
F-2	*Ease of finding merit -base-d job under protective environment of J&K*	
S-4	I have better chances of success in J&K because of less competition owing to special privileges given to J&K state subjects.	2.97
S-5	Because of my academic merit & abilities, it will not be difficult for me to get a govt. Job in J&K.	3.21
F-3	*Perceptions of compromise borne out of exclusivity*	
S-6	J&K offers fewer opportunities for career growth as compared to rest of India.	3.90
S-7	It is very difficult for students of J&K to compete with students at all- India level.	3.24

Source: Author.
(The factor values of the generated factors can be supplied on request.)

5

The Role of Personality Traits, Social Competence, Impression Management and Entrepreneurial Orientation in Entrepreneurial Success

– *Resmi Ann Thomas*
T.J. Kamalanabahan

Introduction

Researchers have been exploring entrepreneurship from varied disciplines, agreeing and disagreeing on the psychological, sociological, economic and environmental concepts. The study of entrepreneurial behaviour is one of the most fascinating and multi-faceted topics imaginable.

An entrepreneur is a person who has possession over a new enterprise or venture and assumes full accountability for the inherent risks and the outcome. Some observers see them as willing to accept a high level of personal, professional or financial risk to pursue that opportunity, but the emerging evidence indicates they are more passionate experts than gamblers. A commonly accepted description of entrepreneurship is "a process of identifying, evaluating and seizing an opportunity, and bringing together all the resources necessary for its success, by devoting time and effort".

However, today's research emphasises the need of a more elaborate and focused definition of entrepreneurship, such as "a scholarly field that seeks to understand how opportunities to bring into existence 'future' goods and services are discovered, created, and exploited, by whom, and with what consequences" (Baron and Markman 2003). Entrepreneurship can be studied within a framework that describes why it is studied, why opportunities exist, why some and not others recognise these opportunities and, finally, how the opportunities are exploited (Shane and Venkataraman 2000; Stevenson and Jarillo 1990). This area is highly under-researched and has potential to answer several questions regarding traits, behaviour and cognition of entrepreneurs.

An answer to this question explored the need for social competencies and social capital (Baron and Markman 2003), which may act as a basis of entrepreneurial success or failure. Even though entrepreneurship is a personal process, success and failure are likely to be partially dictated by personality and genetics, by better understanding the skills, traits, and behaviours that shape the thought process. One can comprehend and map success/failure or at the minimum, have a better understanding of the pitfalls of entrepreneurial thinking (Bender and Hill 2007).

Social competence

In simple terms, an entrepreneur's ability to interact effectively with others is based on discrete social skills can be referred to as "social competence" (Baron and Markman 2003). This summary term is comprised of persuasion, social adaptability, impression management and social perception (ibid.) This encapsulates the combined effects of various social skills such as the ability to perceive others accurately, make a good first impression and persuade others to change their views or behaviour (Wayne and Kacmar 1991). Social skills and social capital define social competence, which is the ability to interact effectively with others, as based on discrete social skills (Baron and Markman 2003).

Social skills are an integral part of social interaction process. The entrepreneur uses this from a wide range of angles in all the stages of firm development, maintenance and performance. The skill sets are inevitable for all the entrepreneurial activities such as raising capital, generating enthusiasm and commitment in others (e.g., employees, partners, customers), communicating effectively with people from a wide range of backgrounds, selecting effective partners and employees, developing networks and relationships, establishing trust and legitimacy (Aldrich and Fiol 1994), and negotiating with others over diverse issues (Baron and Markman 2000).

Social skills are needed to develop entrepreneurial networks, and an entrepreneur's social competence can never be neglected, whether they are built in or acquired. These aspects are always related to the success or failure of an entrepreneurial venture. Social competence has been found to be imperative in the early phase of venture creation when investors have to be persuaded to provide capital. It is also found that cooperation may be augmented when the entrepreneur and venture capitalist share a positive social or business relationship (Cable and Shane 1997). Usually, an entrepreneur's self-presentation includes information about a new opportunity and effective presentation provides a signal to investors about his/her ability to successfully develop and manage a new venture (Feldman and March 1981; Mason and Harrison 2000). Developing social skills such as perception, impression management, persuasiveness, social adaptability, expressiveness, and emotional intelligence could yield large dividends in the capital market (Baron and Markman 2003). Totally, social competence helps to expand networks, build business relationships and alliances, and provide competitive advantages through privileged information (ibid.). It may be found that ideal entrepreneur-venture capitalists' relationship rests on the entrepreneur who can personally impresses the venture capitalist (MacMillan et al. 1985). It is also interesting to note that the inter-personal style and skills of the entrepreneur make the difference in this relationship (Hisrich and Jancowicz 1990). Likewise, creating a negative impression has shown to fall short in selling the business opportunity to investors, and curb investment potential (Mason and Harrison 2000).

Impression management

Impression management is defined in the literature as the process by which individuals attempt to control the impressions others form of them (Leary and Kowalski 1990; Rosenfeld et al. 1995).

Social psychologists have provided both theoretical and empirical evidence for impression management. In his ground breaking work, "The Presentation of Self in Everyday Life," Goffman (1963) interpreted social behaviour, in terms borrowed from the theatre. He proposed that all the people can be viewed as social actors who engage in performances conveying favourable impressions, to please an audience in order to maintain routine social interactions.All behaviour of individuals has the potential of having effect on the impressions others form of them. This means that, in a very broad way, all behaviour can be seen as impression management. And it can be assumed that the actor actively tries to create a relevant impression and is aware of engaging in this process. Evolutionary psychologists assert that strategic impression management is inevitable in evolutionary adaptation through maintaining relationships for mating, friendship and status hierarchies (Koenig and Nezlek 2004). Tedeschi (1984) draws attention to the deliberateness of controlling the impressions. But researchers also argue that impression management need not be a deliberate conscious process, but it still meets its purpose of managing the needed impressions. Darby and Schlenker (1982) demonstrated that even small children engage in self-presentational behaviour.

Motivation for impression management

Social psychologists thrust on the goals of gaining social approval and developing desired identities. Leary and Kowalski (1990) identified three inter-related but distinct goals of impression management. First of all, self-presentation can increase the probability of reaching the desired outcomes. The second goal is enhancing one's self-esteem. In most theories of social behaviour, it is established that people act to restore and maximise their self-esteem (Swann 1996). The third goal is in facilitating the development of identities.

Impression management techniques

Impression management envelops a broad range of behaviour, ranging from choosing a dress one wears (Peluchette et al. 2006), to being pompous about one's accomplishments. The tactics of impression management can both be non-verbal like showing artefacts (uniforms and medals) and expressive behaviour like hand-shaking, frowns, eye contact, and smiles (Schneider 1981) or verbal behaviour like concessions, refusals, justifications and excuses (Schonbach 1980). Jones and Pittman (1982) were the first to develop the taxonomy of impression management tactics based on the kind of images individuals designed to create. The tactics included were the following: (1) **Ingratiation**, flattery, has the purpose of being seen as likeable and characterised by a want to "fit in". (2) **Self-promotion**, a common self- presentation technique, focuses on creating an image of competence. (3) **Exemplification** refers to people who manage the impressions of self-sacrifice, going beyond the call of duty, thereby projecting images of integrity, social responsibility, moral worthiness and dedication. (4) **Intimidation** means tactics of gesturing power or the competence to punish others, with the purpose of being seen as dangerous. (5) **Supplication** refers to tactics aimed at creating a needy or pitiful image by means of demonstrating weakness and incompetence. It is also seen that this technique is most advantageous when the supplicant portrays the deficiencies as temporary. **Self-glorification,** which constitutes self-esteem maintenance and self- construction compensation, has been studied by Schlenker and Weigold (1992). It is an attempt to promote and maintain a positive image. It can be associated with boasting. Paulhus (1984) conceptualised impression management as a component of desirable responding along with self-deceptive enhancement. **Self-deceptive enhancement** or exaggerated self-description (Paulhus et al. 2003) is the tendency of individuals to systematically evaluate themselves as overtly positive. **Impression management** refers to the tendency to present oneself deliberately as favourable to others through positive self- descriptions. Another categorisation is that of **high self-monitoring** and **low self-monitoring** (Snyder 1974), by looking into individual differences. Self-monitoring can be characterised as an active attempt to control images and impressions given to others. High self-monitors have a tendency to apply positive impression management tactics, aimed at creating a desired image than low self-monitors (Bolino and Turnley 2003).

A directional classification can be made like upward impression management (superior oriented), downward impression management (subordinate oriented) and lateral impression management (peer oriented).

Success factors of impression management

In real form, the success of any impression management tactic depends on the audience and the presenter's skill of self-presentation. Successful presenters seem to be more natural and at home with the tactic they use than unsuccessful presenters (Godfrey et al. 1986). Impression management works well when it is a background process, without attention and monitoring (Pontari and Schlenker 2000). A combination of verbal and non-verbal styles is also important. Situation based tactics employment may be called the formula for impression management.

Outcomes of social competence and impression management in entrepreneurship

Mastery in social skills is needed for maintaining a successful firm. Researches have established that social perception, impression management, persuasion, manipulativeness, and expressiveness can be associated with entrepreneurial financial success (Baron and Markman 2000). Social psychologists have yielded valuable insights on the different ways that social competence can be managed and mushroomed under impression management. The skill of social perception is inevitable for a good impression regulation since the self-presentation of the person will rely on his/her perception of the audience (Fiske and Taylor 1991). According to some theorists, influence and persuasion are the basic purpose of self-presentation (Jones and Pittman 1982; Gangestad and Snyder 2000). Researches on inter-personal influence have identified behavioural tactics that lead to influence and some of these tactics show strong similarities with impression management tactics (Kipnis et al. 1980; Yukl and Falbe 1990). Impression managers are best in being able to use secret agendas and to manipulate and deceive others (Tedeschi 1984). Emotional expressions are shaped by real and imagined audiences. For example, people smile more when they are imagining enjoyable situations in which they are with other people rather than alone (Fridlund et al. 1990), and are more facially expressive while experiencing emotions when others are present or are imagined to be near (Fridlund 1991). Except for some specific areas of organisational research, the role of impression management has often been overlooked (Rosenfeld et al. 2002). Seemingly less number of researches have been conducted on entrepreneurial impression management. Further research in this context can considerably improve our understanding of the role impression management plays in entrepreneurial process. Knowledge about normative impression management behaviour used by entrepreneurs can assist nascent entrepreneurs in improving their competencies and success probabilities. This acumen can also help individuals who are looking for an entrepreneurial career to determine the right steps to take in the advent of a new venture. Yet, tactful presentation of self of entrepreneurs has not been studied copiously. Though major researches in social competence recognise impression management as a variable, the role of impression management as a significant contributor to entrepreneurial success has not been proved. This may be due to the low reliability the items had produced (Baron and Markman 2003). The success of impression management is mostly based on the style and execution (Gallagher 2007).

This study proposes that when impression management is studied as a strategic, tactful use of impression management technique, a more reliable picture of the association can be drawn. Therefore, the purpose of the study is to extend the research on the use of impression management in an entrepreneurial context by exploring the relationship between firm performance (success or failure) and the entrepreneur's expressions of impression management tactics.

There are three underlying assumptions to this study:

- Entrepreneurs choose impression management strategies to maximise their personal gain, assuming that a more favourable impression will eventually yield positive outcomes.

- Entrepreneurs tend to show situations demanding impression management tactics.
- Impression management is significantly associated with entrepreneurial success.

Entrepreneurial success and related concepts

The predictors of entrepreneurial success have been widely researched all through the years. The role of entrepreneur-associated factors (like personality, motivation, risk taking, opportunity identification, proactiveness, innovation, networking and demographic variables), firm- associated factors (like capital, market opportunities and financial approach of the firm) and external factors (location, etc.) have been pondered. Psychologists are still musing over the personality and behavioural patterns of entrepreneurship. There are studies focusing on entrepreneurs' personalities, backgrounds, early experiences (Carland et al. 1984), and in some traits have been widely criticised and have generally produced disappointing findings (Low and Macmillan 1988; Gartner 1990). Though conflicting theories questioning the need of studying the personality of entrepreneurs exist, the very fact that personality forms the basis of all human demeanours cannot be overlooked.

Holland (1985) has assessed and described six vocational personality types, each with a different set of work-related characteristics, abilities, and interests. One of these is the Entrepreneurial (E-) type. Entrepreneurial types flourish in work environments that involve and reward the ability to convince, direct, and manipulate others; competition, initiative in the pursuit of financial or material accomplishment, dominance, self-confidence; and a sense for managerial, sales, and business-related issues. This classification holds good for the need of social competencies that should be possessed by the entrepreneur in order to be successful.

Therefore the entrepreneur can best be identified with the presence of some basic personality traits like need for achievement, need for dominance, and need for autonomy.

Need for achievement

McClelland (1965) has pioneered in this area, using Thematic Apperception Tests (TATs), and discovering that entrepreneurs scored high on need for achievement. Roberts (1968) and Wainer and Rubin (1969), who investigated the relationship between successful research and development (R&D) entrepreneurs and company performance, found that the highest performing companies were led by entrepreneurs with high need for achievement and moderate need for power, as measured by projective TAT tests. Similarly, Hornaday and Aboud (1971), using objective personality measures, reported that entrepreneurs scored significantly higher on achievement and independence than the population in general.

Need for achievement can also be correlated with impression management techniques such that, in a leadership oriented study, Mowday et al. (1979) found that need for achievement and need for power were positively related to the propensity to engage in influential tactics in an organisation. Leaders with high need for achievement would engage in impression management to bolster their image of competence and success (House 1977; Bass 1985).

Need for dominance

Given an operating environment that is not conducive to entrepreneurial activity, applying one's skills successfully may create a sense of power for the entrepreneur.

Persons high on need for power, as portrayed by McClelland (1953), have a desire to control, to be responsible for others and to influence others' behaviour (Cherrington 1989). These individuals are characterised with the tendency to make suggestions, give opinions, and attempt to persuade, seek active leadership roles and strive to gain control over events (Steers and Braunstein 1976). Mowday (1978) found that persons high in need for power were more likely to engage in upward influence activities (such as threats, legitimate authority, persuasive arguments, rewards or exchange of favours, and covert manipulation). These people are less likely to use ingratiation (Caldwell and Burger 1997). In the organisational setting, people with high need for dominance are found to use competence tactics. Most of the research on impression management is confined in the area of organisational citizenship behaviour, political skill and leadership; the area of entrepreneurship is highly under-researched.

Need for autonomy

Entrepreneurs are often characterised and described as independent people, mainly due to the fact that they do not want to be in a conforming situation. Most of them leave the comfort of their jobs to start a venture independently, willing to take all the risks and troubles lying ahead. Cromie and O'sullivan (1999) have held that entrepreneurs are people who do not like to obey the rules and regulations of organisations.

Need for autonomy or autonomy orientation can be linked with impression management, like any other dispositional characteristics. Need for autonomy has not been explored in impression management literature as much as locus of control. But it can be assumed that people with high desire to be independent will engage in self-promotional and self-glorification tactics rather than supplication.

Need for affiliation

The very fact that need for autonomy and need for affiliation are contradicting characteristics, and that researchers are still arguing about the level and presence of affiliation needs in an entrepreneur's life, makes it a very interesting concept for research. Generally, individuals with high affiliative needs are not concerned with task accomplishments unless they are instrumental in building inter-personal relationships (Atkinson and Reitman 1965). Studies have shown that individuals with a moderate need for affiliation tend to be more effective managers and helpers than those with high or low affiliation (Boyatzis 1974). Wainer and Rubin (1969) have found association between high need for affiliation and successful entrepreneurs. Jain and Triandis (1997) have also stated the role of affiliation in establishing and maintaining relationships that acts as a basis of entrepreneurial success.

Researches in impression management have found that persons who are agreeable are similar to those who have a high need for affiliation in that they are also more trusting, caring, gentle, and even compliant (Perrewé and Spector 2002). Likewise, highly agreeable persons are more likely to build relationships, encourage cooperation, and show consideration for others (Witt et al. 2002). Hence, it follows that persons high in need for affiliation will be more likely to engage in ingratiation in an effort to build networks and manipulative relations. Moreover, persons high in need for affiliation will be more likely to use supplication.

Entrepreneurial orientation

A skill centred entrepreneurial orientation, that combines the dispositional traits and behaviour of entrepreneurs have been found to be a precursor of entrepreneurial performance. Entrepreneurial orientation should be distinguished from entrepreneurship, which is related to new business entry and is concerned primarily with questions such as "What business do we enter?" and "How do we make the new business succeed?" (Richard et al. 2004). Entrepreneurial orientation is a process that constructs and concerns the "methods, practices, and decision making styles managers use" (Lumpkin and Dess 1996). In their entrepreneurial career, according to Match (1991), an entrepreneur will have to acquire and develop basic practice-oriented management competence and skills to be required for strategic planning and implementation, resource allocation, and relationship maintenance throughout the stages of their business.

Miller (1983) has analysed the four dimensions of EO approximating on innovativeness, risk taking, proactiveness, and competitive aggressiveness. But many researchers have identified and tested only three of the dimensions of EO: innovativeness, risk taking, proactiveness. Anumber of studies have addressed competitive aggressiveness by equating it with pro-activeness (Covin and Slevin 1989).

Innovativeness is held as a basic property of entrepreneurial functions, one that looks into the entrepreneur's willingness to adopt novel ways away from the existing ones, the enthusiasm to assume pioneering ideas and methods into their venture operations, and the eagerness to implement the innovative strategy.

Pro-activeness can be considered as a response to opportunities, in that the entrepreneur tries to find the market opportunities away from the entrepreneurs' present style of operation (Venkataraman 1997). It can be linked as a part of innovative methodology.

Risk taking is a term long associated with entrepreneurship, with variations in the definitions that entrepreneurs are moderate risk takers (Cunningham and Lischeron 1991), that entrepreneurs are calculated risk takers (Brockhaus 1980) and also that entrepreneurs tend to engage in more risk taking activities than non-entrepreneurs (Falbe and Larwood 1995).

Relevance of social competence and impression management in EO

The role of social skills in entrepreneurial orientation has still not been explored much (Bender and Hill 2007). Entrepreneurial orientation is characterised by opportunity recognition, risk assumption and finding innovative methods to utilise the opportunity. This becomes the minimum qualification to become an entrepreneur, and thus the basis of entrepreneurial function. In this stance, the need for social competence and skills in networking, persuasion and impression management, social adaptability, communication, etc., have been proved to be yielding entrepreneurial success (Baron and Markman 2000; Baron and Markman 2003; Bender and Hill 2007). The study proposes that proper and tactful presentation of impression management techniques by an entrepreneur with high entrepreneurial orientation would prove imperative in determining the success and failure of entrepreneurs. The study also assumes that entrepreneurs might use any impression management technique, not just competence related (intimidation, self-promotion and self- glorification), but also conformity related (ingratiation, supplication) in order to be successful.

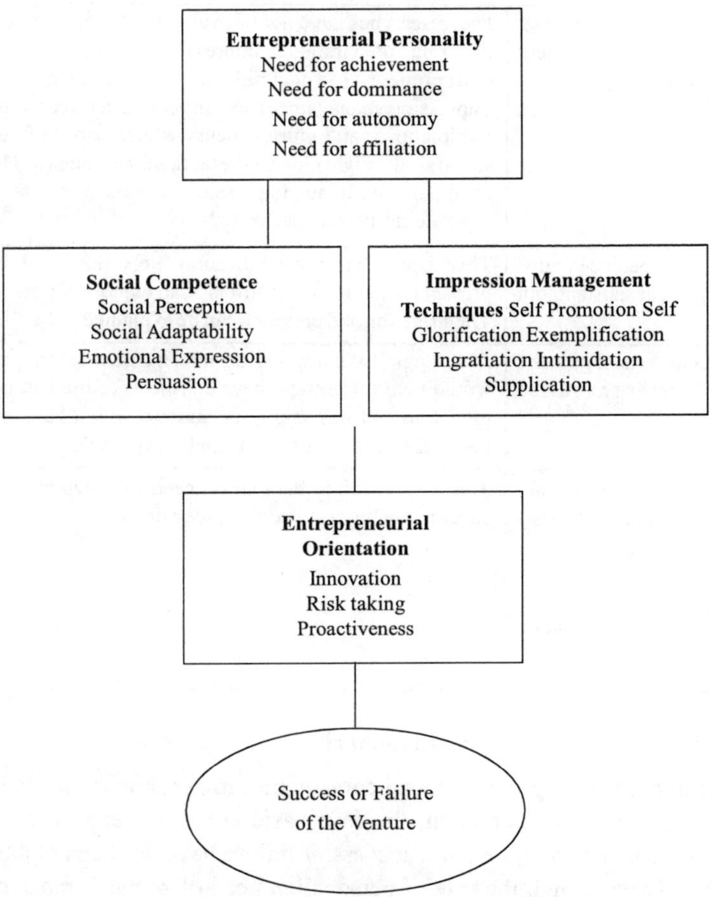

Fig. 5.1: Conceptualised model.

Nut shell...

Concepts connected	*Rationale*
Personality traits and social competence	Personality traits have been found to dictate the development and use of social skills. The role of entrepreneural specific traits on social competence can be explained and reaffirmed.
Personality traits and impression management	Personality traits are the major precursor in determing the type of impression management techniques used by the entrepreneur. This field needs to be researched and examined.
Social competence and impression management techniques	Past researches have not been able to clearly point out the role of strategic impression management in entrepreneurial financial success. The use of impression management techniques differ according to situations, and entrepreneurs whose core high on social skills might change the tactics consequently.The need for studying impression management as a separate entity can be affirmed.
Social competence and entrepreneurialorientation	This aspect has not been completely pondered by present researchers and still is at an exploratory stage. Their relation and presence can be explained.
Impression manage ment and entrepreneurial orientation	A strategic user impression management techniques would help the entrepreneur in aspects of innovation, proactive and risk taking behaviour, which have not been researched.This facet can be explored.
Personality traits, social competence, impression management, entrepreneurial orientation and entrepreneurial success or failure.	The decisive roll of the four concepts in entrepreneurial success can be explored and ascertained.

Importance of the proposed research

Entrepreneurial persona, social competence, impression management and entrepreneurial orientation, the four basic concepts decisive to the understanding of entrepreneur's success or failure have not been clubbed together. Even though the role of personality, need of social competence and presence of entrepreneurial orientation have been treated exploratively, impression management, which is widely recognised as one of the prerequisite of entrepreneurial success is not yet highlighted. Combining situation and tactic specific impression management technique in the paradigm would certainly yield much explicit results. Entrepreneurs who have lagged behind in their journey can be helped with this insight and future entrepreneurs can approach their venture with better awareness.

Blending the possibilities offered by this research with the fact of increasing number of entrepreneurial firms in India, it becomes more important to comprehend the dynamics involved in impression management and establishing its implications.

6

Effect of Gender on Inception Stage of Entrepreneurs: Evidence from Small and Micro Enterprises in Indore

– Meghna Chhabra
Yamini Karmarkar

Abstract

In common perception it is taken for granted that entrepreneurs driven by some internal motivation simply emerge. But, little is known about the king of obstacles they face at the inception stage. Entrepreneurship comes with a host of rewarding challenges. This study aims at analysing the obstacles faced by entrepreneurs at the inception stage of their businesses and the gender related distinctiveness in the same. The research design is descriptive in nature and has been carried out primarily by using survey method. The universe of the study is based on the list of all small and micro business units initiated and developed by male and female entrepreneurs in Indore city and the sample size is 500. The 'Obstacles faced at inception stage' included eleven variables; not faced any obstacle, question of self-confidence, difficulty in raising start-up finance, lack of information/advice on how to start a business, difficult to find right contacts for business, no awareness/access to business support, lacked management skills, lacked entrepreneurial skills, lacked inter-cultural and language skills for foreign markets, difficult to combine family and work life and faced gender discrimination. Percentage analysis was used to analyse the 'Obstacles faced at inception stage' by male and female entrepreneurs. ANOVA was run for "Gender" of entrepreneur and eleven variables of 'Obstacles faced at inception stage' to ascertain the effect of gender on these variables. Maximum number of entrepreneurs have attributed "difficulty in raising start-up finance" as the biggest obstacle. Alongside, there is a drastic difference in the number of female entrepreneurs, as compared to their male counterparts, who believe that they were unable to strike a work/life balance while starting their business. Therefore, public policy to promote entrepreneurship needs to be tailored carefully to different groups.

Introduction

The emergence and development of entrepreneurship is a significant phenomenon in contemporary economies. Entrepreneurship is strongly linked to micro and small enterprises, which are the main developing force of the developing economies. Having this in mind, the research problem here is connected with questioning what are the obstacles faced at inception stage by entrepreneurs in a developing country and does a gender gap exist in this perspective. These factors have considerable impact on success and failure rates of these entrepreneurs and their survival rates.

Literature review

The most commonly researched environmental restraint for start-ups is availability of capital and biased (gender) attitude of bank loan officers. In an early study, Buttner and Rosen (1988) found that bank loan officers perceived men to be more "entrepreneurial" than women – men were rated higher in leadership, autonomy, risk-taking propensity, readiness for change, and endurance. Men were also perceived to be less emotional and to have a lower need for support, leading the authors to conclude that sex stereotyping existed. The same authors found in a loan decision simulation a year later that gender did not influence bank loan officers' decisions (Buttner & Rosen 1989). Riding and Swift (1990) found in a large Canadian study that banks had higher collateral requirements for women. Interest rates did not differ. They also found that a lower percentage of women than men had a line of credit, leading them to conclude that the banking relationships seemed more difficult for women. Buttner and Rosen (1992), referring to their previous studies, noted that women often claimed to be discriminated against even though research did not fully support this. They hypothesised that there were gender differences in perceptions. They surveyed male and female entrepreneurs with a hypothetical situation in which they were denied a loan. They found no difference in estimates of the difficulty of getting a loan and no significant difference in the rankings of reasons for denial as a function of gender, age or experience. There were no significant differences in post- denial strategies either – women were actually more prone to seek venture capital.

Brush (1997) inquired into women's own opinions as well. She asked a set of eight female entrepreneurs in a focus group study what they alleged to be the opportunities and obstacles for woman entrepreneurs. Child and dependent care, being taken seriously, lack of female role models in entrepreneurship education and access to growth capital were the stated obstacles. Three opportunities were mentioned: women's participative management style, modern genderless information technology and women's holistic employee policies.

A woman might even use one of these "barriers" to compensate for the other according to Carter et al. (1997:127), who wrote, "We test whether dispositional characteristics can be used to overcome or moderate deficiencies that arise from situational differences". The idea was that a woman could use her relational skills (a result of the dispositional barriers) and use a funding tactic with a competitive advantage in comparison to those without such skills, which would balance for her lack of education or experience, i.e., the situational barriers. In this stream of thinking, even structural factors become an individual responsibility.

Marlow (1997) found when comparing a matched sample of men and woman entrepreneurs that only women found it difficult to combine work and family. As for suggestions of how to remedy the situation, men had few such, and the women offered only "privatised" solutions to what was in fact, as Marlow puts it, group subordination. The women suggested, for example, hard work, visible financial success and sharing domestic responsibility with the family. ...if women are utilising self-employment as a solution to dual demands of domestic and waged labour, then the experience of self-employment is tainted by patriarchal expectations. Moreover, if women perceive that the solutions to such issues lie in privatised, individual effort or merit to achieve within existing scales of judgement, small firm ownership will reflect the subordination evident in other areas of women's lives (Marlow 1997:208).

The fundamental idea in most researches in the field of women entrepreneurship is that it is not the manner in which individual woman is constituted that is problematic and a possible restraint to growth, but rather their lesser access to relevant business education and entrepreneurial or managerial experience. Having a family might also be regarded as a structural feature. The results are, as mentioned before, full of loopholes, but what is significantly striking is that even if these so called structural features are put forward as explanations, the therapy is envisioned as individual. Either individual women are suggested to get the right education, or policy makers are advised to organise entrepreneurship training for women. It can be labeled as individual adjustment to existing structures, not structural transformation.

Rationale of the study

Despite current economic advances, India's gender balance for entrepreneurship remains among the lowest in the world. Improving this balance is an important step for India's development and its achievement of gender equality and greater economic growth. There is comparatively less extensive literature available in entrepreneurial research arena in relation to the subject of Gender Gap. In view of escalating global entrepreneurial scenario, more substantial research on this issue is the need of the hour.

Indore is the largest city of the Indian state of Madhya Pradesh and the most populous metropolitan area in central India. Indore exerts a significant impact upon commerce, finance, media, art, fashion, research, technology, education, and entertainment and has been described as the commercial capital of the central India. Major industrial areas surrounding the city include the Sanwer Industrial belt and the Pithampur special economic zone. While trading and textile manufacturing are the oldest businesses contributing to economy, the real estate business has emerged very fast in the past few years.

The city has undergone tremendous entrepreneurial growth in the past decade with various new malls with fresh brand outlets, food courts and multiplexes. Treasure city, which finds its origin here, is acclaimed to be the biggest mall of central India. Infosys is setting up a new development centre at Indore with an investment of Rs 100 crore in phase one at the super corridor. Collabera and TCS have also announced plans for opening campuses in Indore. The MP government has also done the land allotment. Besides these, there are several medium and small size software development firms in Indore. It is gaining pace as the tier-II city of India. The city offers immense entrepreneurial prospects owing to the following reasons: centrally located, commercial capital of central India with moderate and pleasant climate, high quality lifestyle with low cost, quality housing facility at reasonable rate, significant number of good hotels, multiplexes, clubs, shopping malls, world class medical facilities available (Bombay Hospital, CHL Apollo, many more), educational hub of central India with a number of prominent engineering/management colleges and english medium schools, Centre for Advanced Technology (CAT). A huge reservoir of economic and skilled manpower - nearly 70,000 graduates including 15,000 technical graduates - are available every year; no labour issues, lockouts or closures in the city; it is the 'Soyabean' capital of the country and having National Soyabean Research Centre, excellent connectivity with the entire country and abroad through rail, road and air transport, advanced telecommunications network through BSNL, VSNL, Idea, Airtel, Reliance, Tata Indicom and Vodaphone. The city offers high quality social infrastructure, low cost and easy availability of land as compared to other parts of the country.

With the advent of higher entrepreneurial activities the number of woman-owned businesses along with woman involved businesses are constantly on the rise. Such businesses are ranging from garments to health and fitness centres, textiles to beauty, food processing to manufacturing, education to handicrafts, and provide more and more options for women. Recent years have witnessed an increase in such a trend thereby resulting in increased women participation as 'entrepreneurs' and as 'employees', and also in due course making provision of employment opportunities for a number of young women from semi-urban and rural areas. Hence Indore is well equipped to gather adequate responses to study the 'obstacles faced at inception stage' of male and female entrepreneurs and to identify the gender gap, if any, in the aforesaid 'obstacles faced at inception stage'.

Problem formulation

The micro sector with 14.85 lakh working enterprises, accounts for 94.94 per cent of working enterprises of MSME sector and is the most dominant segment in terms of number of enterprises. This sector also accounts for the largest and a very dominant share of employment (70.19%) by registered MSME sector. Further, the micro sector with 44.24 per cent share of gross output of MSME sector is only marginally short of the share of small sector (45.06%), which has the highest sectorial share within the registered MSME sector. Small sector with 0.76 lakh enterprises accounts for 4.89 per cent of working enterprises in the MSME sector, but for less than 5 per cent of enterprises in the registered MSME sector. The data clearly indicates the current trend towards entrepreneurial ventures, which is growing day by day. But the differences in the 'business practices' of the entrepreneurs based on gender need to be evaluated. Also, it is important to analyse if there is a gender gap in the 'obstacles faced at inception stage' by these entrepreneurs, what that gap is and what its repercussions are. In comparison, less research has been done in the relevant context in India. Hence this particular study tries to understand the gender gap in the 'obstacles faced at inception stage' of the entrepreneurs in small and micro enterprises in India. The 'obstacles faced at inception stage' included eleven variables: not faced any obstacle, question of self-confidence, difficulty in raising start-up finance, lack of information/advice on how to start a business, difficult to find right contacts for business, no awareness/ access to business support, lacked management skills, lacked entrepreneurial skills, lacked inter-cultural and language skills for foreign markets, difficult to combine family and work life and faced gender discrimination. These variables were measured on 'ordinal'scale.

Objectives of the study

The present study is descriptive, done on male and female entrepreneurs in India. The micro and small businesses started/owned by male and female entrepreneurs were included in the sample. The specific objectives of the study were as follows:

- To study the 'obstacles faced at inception stage' of selected entrepreneurs of small and micro enterprises in terms of the eleven variables identified.
- To study the "gender gap", if any, among 'obstacles at inception stage' faced by selected entrepreneurs of small and micro enterprises.

Research methodolgy

This research aimed at studying the 'obstacles at inception stage'of male and female entrepreneurs of micro and small enterprises in Indore and the gender gap, if any, in the aforesaid variables. The universe of the study was based on the list of all small and micro business units initiated and developed by male and female entrepreneurs in Indore city. The research has been carried out primarily by using survey method. The units of observation were the entrepreneurs of micro and small enterprises.

Sample size

As the study is primarily based in Indore and surrounding areas, male and female entrepreneurs of micro and small business sector there were selected for the study. As per the research conducted by MSME Development Institute, Indore, the total number of micro and small enterprises in manufacturing, service and retail in Indore were found to be 12,705. To determine the sample size, using the Creative Research Systems software, the total number of 12,705 was taken as population, and confidence level of 95 per cent and confidence interval of 4. The result was 573 enterprises which were in actuality implemented as 500.

Data collection

The survey method was used for collecting primary data. The survey was conducted with the help of a structured questionnaire; 1,150 questionnaires were distributed to male and female entrepreneurs, out of which 672 were filled and returned.

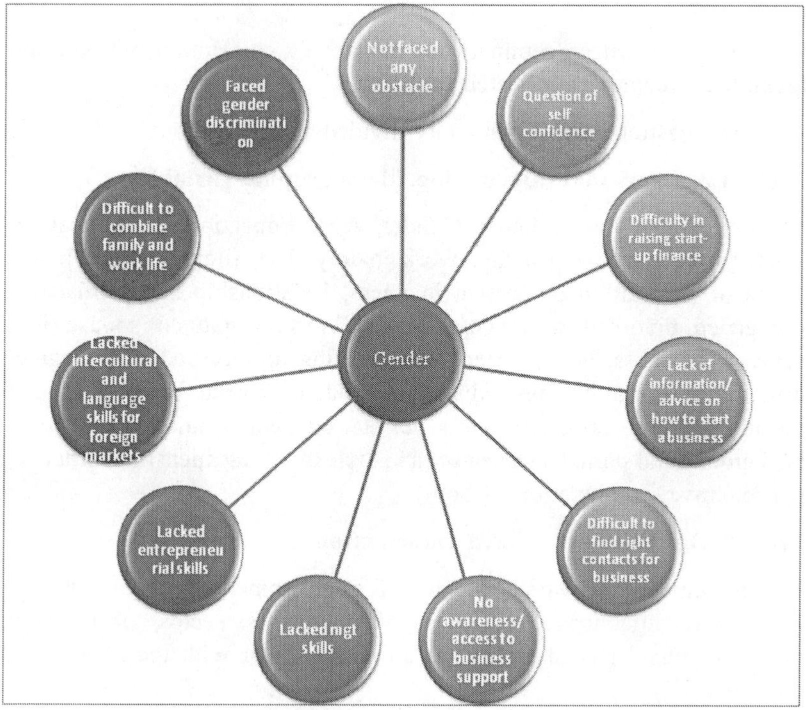

Fig. 6.1: Variables included under 'obstacles at inception stage' of entrepreneurs

Out of them 460 were found relevant for the study (entrepreneurs running enterprises satisfying the definition of micro and small enterprises under the MSMED Act only were considered for study); 150 questionnaires were mailed, 72 were filled and mailed back and 40 were found relevant for the study. Thus primary data was collected from 500 entrepreneurs.

The secondary data was collected from various reports published by GEM (Global Entrepreneurship Monitor), Ministry of Micro, Small and Medium Enterprises, United Nations Industrial Development Organization, central and state governments, journals, books, articles in news-papers,

Table –6. 1: Description of sample

Population size	12,705
Sample size	500
Confidence level	95%
Confidence interval	04
Distributed questionnaires	1150
Received	672
Usable	500

websites, conferences, seminars and magazines, etc. Both qualitative and quantitative data was collected for study.

The questionnaire was broadly divided into 2 sections.

Section A - Personal information (demographic variables)

It included the variables Gender, Age, Educational qualification, Average daily working hours, Work mainly from (home, office, both), Years of association of present business, Relationship status (married, unmarried, divorced, widowed/widower), Working status of spouse (job, separate business, not working, was working now retired/quit, Degree/ diploma in formal business education, Mode of starting business (joined family business, family business yet started own venture, no business background and started own venture and Style of management (authoritative, participative, combination of both).

Section B – Business related Information

It included the variables year of establishment, type of business (service, manufacturing, retail/wholesale), business sector, 'obstacles at inception stage' (listed earlier) as an entrepreneur with the strength of occurrence.

Operational definitions

Woman enterprise

"An enterprise owned and controlled by a women having a minimum financial interest of 51 per cent of the capital and giving at least 51 per cent of the employment generated by the enterprise to women."— Government of India

Woman entrepreneur

"A woman entrepreneur can be defined as a confident, innovative and creative woman capable of achieving self-economic independence individually or in collaboration, generates employment opportunities for others through initiating, establishing and running the enterprise by keeping pace with her personal, family and social life."—Kamal Singh

'Obstacles at inception stage'of the entrepreneurs

These have been already enumerated.

Analysis and results

Obstacles at inception stage

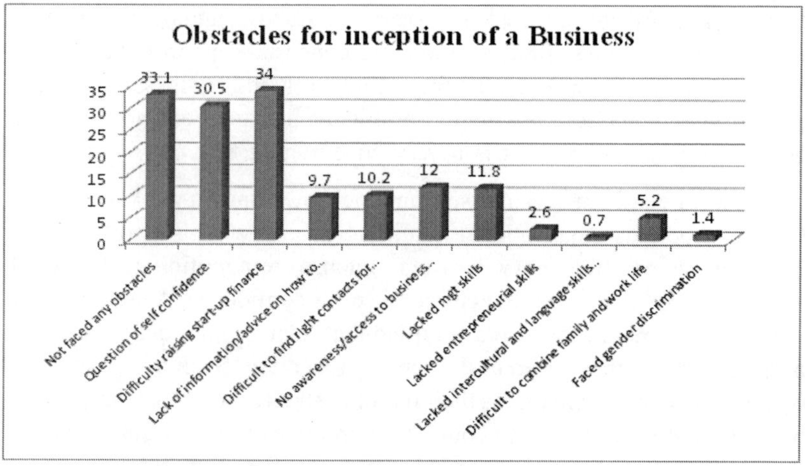

Fig. 6.2: 'Obstacles at inception stage'for male and female entrepreneurs

Maximum number of entrepreneurs (34%) have identified "difficulty in raising start-up finance" as the biggest obstacle they faced at the inception of their business. Start-up finance can be raised from sources such as previous savings, profits from other business and help from family members. External financing sources are finance from lenders, banks and financial institutions, venture capitalists and small investors. Such a high rate of entrepreneurs facing start-up finance obstacle is an alarming fact since there are many schemes and policies initiated by GoI (Government of India) to encourage entrepreneurship in which start-up finance is provided at subsidised rates and is given readily to the deserving new entrepreneurs. Attention must be given by the policy makers to providing such finance, and equal attention must be given and consistent efforts should be made towards creating awareness amongst existing as well as aspiring entrepreneurs about the existence of such schemes that provide finance so that they benefit the maximum number of entrepreneurs. If an entrepreneur who has a brilliant idea, appropriate capabilities, qualification and network and is capable of bearing the entrepreneurial risks is unable to start a business owing to paucity of funds, it is not only a personal loss but the loss created by the pool of such entrepreneurs definitely slows down the pace of economic growth of the nation. Thus it is necessary to attract the attention of the policy makers towards this problem.

Of the total, 33.1 per cent of the entrepreneurs quoted that they did not face any obstacles at the time of inception of their business, which is good news pointing towards the growth and development of an 'entrepreneur friendly atmosphere' where a new and a budding entrepreneur while starting business finds a good entrepreneurial support system in the form of start-up finance, availability of network and business support, is able to effectively combine family and work life and does not face any gender discrimination. This is a very encouraging fact.

Lack of confidence can arise from one's own known weaknesses like lack of experience, educational qualification and weak support system. External factors like entry barriers, intense competition and market dynamism can also affect the entrepreneurial confidence. A high number of entrepreneurs (30.5%) have admitted that 'lack of confidence' was the biggest obstacle they faced at the time of inception. Such a high number of entrepreneurs stating this as their major obstacle, shows that there might be many more persons who could be entrepreneurs but could not be as they lacked confidence in their skills and abilities. Can entrepreneurial confidence be inculcated? Yes, by providing platforms and forums for discussions of their inhibitions. A new idea can be to impart entrepreneurial counselling and for that the mentors can be existing entrepreneurs and academicians specialising in entrepreneurship.

About 12 per cent of the entrepreneurs stated that their major obstacle at the time of inception of their business was their lack of awareness and subsequent lack of access to any kind of business support in the form of direct and indirect assistance from government and non-government institutions. Management skills comprise of leadership and people management, communication skills, collaboration skills, business management skills, finance skills and project management skills: 11.8 per cent of entrepreneurs indicated lack of these skills as their major hurdle while in inception. A business network of contacts is both a route to market for the entrepreneur, and a marketing method. Business networking is a way for him/her to make the maxim, "It's not what you know, it's who you know" work for him/her. It is an effective low-cost marketing method for developing sales opportunities and contacts, based on referrals and introductions - either face-to-face at meetings and gatherings, or by other contact methods such as phone, email, and increasingly social and business networking websites. Futher, 10.2 per cent of the entrepreneurs admitted that they could not develop such networks and thus were unable to find the right contacts of business.

When starting a business, an entrepreneur needs information on varied sources like finance, taxes, technology, licences, markets, vendors, competition, etc. Besides he/she also needs to find out if there were specific rules and regulations that apply to each state or territory that they operated in. About 9.7 per cent of the entrepreneurs did not possess any information/advice on how to start a business. Balancing work and home responsibilities is a challenge for most people. An entrepreneur should make work and family balance a conscious decision. Understanding this can reduce frustration and help him/ her act to gain control. Fortunately, a lesser percentage of entrepreneurs (5.2%) found inability of maintaining such a balance as their major obstacle when starting the business.

An entrepreneur needs to be optimistic and resilient. Their good inter-personal skills include good communication, leadership and motivation. Besides they need to be creative and critical in business knowledge and decision making. About 2.6 per cent of the entrepreneurs admitted a lack of such entrepreneurial skills as the major block while their business was in inception. Only 1.4 per cent of the entrepreneurs faced gender discrimination while starting their business, which is good news as this percentage is small. But still policy makers need to pay attention to eradicating even this much discrimination in order to induce a healthy entrepreneurial scenario in the nation; 0.7 per cent of the entrepreneurs felt that their major obstacle while starting the business was that they lacked interest and language skills for foreign markets.

Effect of gender : ANOVA

Analysis of variance (ANOVA) is a collection of statistical models used in order to analyse the differences between group means and their associated procedures (such as "variation" among and between groups).

Table - 6.2: ANOVA for Gender of entrepreneur and obstacles faced

		Sum of squares	*df*	*Mean Square*	*F*	*Sig.*
"Not faced any obstacle"	Between groups	245.476	1	245.476	13.116	.000
	Within groups	6400.617	342	18.715		
	Total	6646.093	343			
"Question of self-confidence"	Between groups	15.718	1	15.718	2.574	.110
	Within groups	2112.662	346	6.106		
	Total	2128.379	347			
"Difficulty in raising start-up finance"	Between groups	4.960	1	4.960	.886	.347
	Within groups	1915.494	342	5.601		
	Total	1920.453	343			
"Lack of information/advice on how to start a business"	Between groups	84.987	1	84.987	14.092	.000
	Within groups	1845.464	306	6.031		
	Total	1930.451	307			
"Difficult to find right contacts for business"	Between groups	7.326	1	7.326	1.350	.246
	Within groups	1741.888	321	5.426		
	Total	1749.214	322			
"No awareness/ access to business support"	Between groups	29.579	1	29.579	5.962	.015
	Within groups	1438.763	290	4.961		
	Total	1468.342	291			
"Lacked mgt skills"	Between groups	5.269	1	5.269	.632	.427
	Within groups	2666.246	320	8.332		
	Total	2671.516	321			
"Lacked entrepreneurial skills"	Between groups	72.459	1	72.459	14.063	.000
	Within groups	1597.221	310	5.152		
	Total	1669.679	311			
"Lacked inter-cultural and language skills for foreign markets"	Between groups	19.202	1	19.202	3.782	.053
	Within groups	1426.657	281	5.077		
	Total	1445.859	282			
"Difficult to combine family and work life"	Between groups	110.352	1	110.352	12.	.001
	Within groups	2821.978	307	9.192		
	Total	2932.330	308			
"Faced gender discrimination"	Between groups	626.028	1	626.028	108.436	.000
	Within groups	1639.608	284	5.773		
	Total	2265.636	285			

ANOVA was run for gender of entrepreneur and the eleven variables of 'obstacles at inception stage' to ascertain whether there was any significant effect of gender on these variables.

If significant value is less than 0.5, then there is a significant relationship. Out of 11 variables seven variables were: found to have significant relationship with gender. These variables were not faced any obstacle, lack of information/advice on how to start a business, no awareness/

access to business support, lacked entrepreneurial skills, lacked intercultural and language skills for foreign markets, difficult to combine family and work life and faced gender discrimination. Four variables were not found to have any significant relationship with gender. Thus there is a gender gap in the aforesaid seven variables.

If the gender gap existed in the aforesaid seven variables, what was that gender gap? Answers to this question are given in the following chart comprised of comparable percentages for male, female and total entrepreneurs for each of the seven variables.

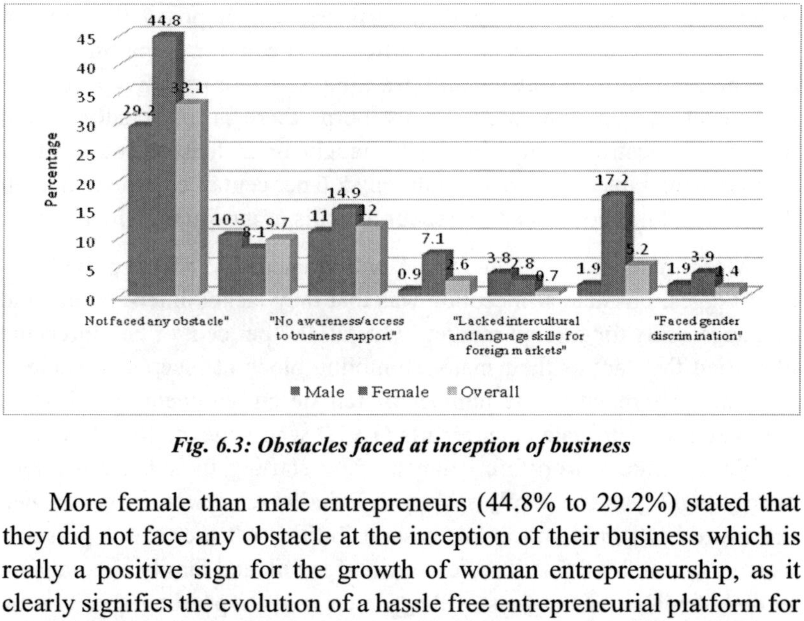

Fig. 6.3: Obstacles faced at inception of business

More female than male entrepreneurs (44.8% to 29.2%) stated that they did not face any obstacle at the inception of their business which is really a positive sign for the growth of woman entrepreneurship, as it clearly signifies the evolution of a hassle free entrepreneurial platform for women. The overall of 38.1 per cent entrepreneurs who did not face any obstacle at inception is also a very healthy sign pointing towards an escalating entrepreneurial support system. More male entrepreneurs (10.3%) than female entrepreneurs (8.1%) have observed that they lacked information and advice on how to start a business and this became their biggest obstacle during inception. Again it signifies the emergence of more informed woman entrepreneurs with better networks of advice and assistance than their male counterparts. Overall 9.7 per cent of entrepreneurs mentioned this as their major stumbling block at inception.

On the contrary, more female (14.9%) than male (11%) entrepreneurs felt absence of awareness of/access to business support provided by various government and non-government institutions as their major hurdle at inception. If only they had been aware of the existence of such support and had used them, their business plans could have taken a different leap. Therefore, there is a dire need for making such policies and programmes more useful for woman entrepreneurs, and the first step towards it is to conduct seminars and programmes wherein such information is flown towards the right channel, i.e., the aspiring entrepreneurs. This is the need of the hour. The overall percentage of such entrepreneurs is 12 per cent. There is a significant difference between the number of male and female entrepreneurs (0.9% as compared to 7.1%), with a higher number of woman entrepreneurs admitting that they did not possess any entrepreneurial skills at the time of starting their business, which posed the greatest difficulty for them. It clearly signifies the need for imparting better entrepreneurship education and training for women. Even for the nomenclature that 'entrepreneurs are born' there is an equally voiced opinion that entrepreneurship can be taught or at least encouraged by entrepreneurship education. Overall only 2.6 per cent of entrepreneurs felt that they did not possess entrepreneurial skills at inception, which is low.

More male (3.8%) than female entrepreneurs (2.8%) reported that their biggest obstacle at inception was that they lacked inter-cultural and language skills for foreign markets. Overall 0.7 per cent of entrepreneurs identified this fact as their major stumbling block at inception. There is a drastic difference in the number of female entrepreneurs (17.2%) as compared to their male counterparts (1.9%) who believed that they were unable to strike a work/life balance while starting their business. This clearly highlights the family system in India where a woman is assigned the entire household and family responsibilities whether she is pursuing a career or not. Men find it easier to balance work and family as compared to their female counterparts as they perceive that spending quality time with the family is sufficient for them to strike a work/family balance. They are not expected to shoulder responsibilities on a daily basis and this makes things smoother for them. Such mindsets and cultural norms need to be changed drastically as it is need of the hour that men start shouldering equally the family and household responsibilities especially when the woman of the house is also pursuing a career and is also a breadwinner for the family. Overall 5.2 per cent of entrepreneurs expressed inability to strike work/life balance as their major hurdle while starting the business.

More female (3.9%) than male (1.9%) entrepreneurs faced gender discrimination in business. This is significant, highlighting the need for development and execution of measures at national as well as regional levels to eradicate such discriminations which are an outcome of mindsets arising out of cultural norms. It is required now that woman entrepreneurship be applauded, respected and sought for as a measure of exploiting the ever so unexploited talents and potentials of woman capital, which is definitely going to fuel up the engine of entrepreneurial growth in the nation. Overall 1.4 per cent of entrepreneurs faced gender discrimination while starting their business.

Out of eleven parameters selected to study the Gender Gap in "obstacles for inception of a business", seven were found to be significantly different for males and females. These were: Not faced any obstacle, Lack of information/advice on how to start a business, No awareness/access to business support, Lacked entrepreneurial skills, Lacked inter-cultural and language skills for foreign markets, Difficult to combine family and work life and Faced gender discrimination. The remaining four parameters namely Question of self confidence, Difficulty in raising start-up finance, Difficult to find right contacts for business, Lacked management skills, were found to be similar for males and females.

Limitations

- The main constraint was designing of common questionnaire for male and female entrepreneurs which highlights their problems and success factors.
- Another constraint was identifying the entrepreneurs belonging to small and micro sectors and coaxing them to share the personal and business information and perceived entrepreneurial experience, which was very difficult and resistance was encountered.
- Lack of studies which identify gender gap in entrepreneurship also was a constraint, as only recently studies began to focus on understanding gender and entrepreneurship at macro level.

7

INNOVATION AND ENTREPRENEURSHIP IN A GLOBAL ECONOMY

– *GIRIJA NANDINI*

Abstract

Innovation is simply "a new way of doing something". As a discipline, innovation is capable of being learned, as well as practised. Innovation consists of the purposeful and organised search for changes and in the systematic analysis of the opportunities such changes might offer for economic or social innovation. In the 1980s large corporate R&D departments as well as academic institutions were the seat of innovation. Now when people want to innovate and be entrepreneurial, they leave the corporate world and set out on their own. They get money for their start-up ventures from a variety of sources, sometimes even mortgaging their homes. Often they take substantial risks to follow their dreams, which is where the term "lifestyle entrepreneur" was born. This paper tries to analyse the conceptual approach to entrepreneurship, the position of innovation and entrepreneurship in India and also its future.

Key words: *Innovation, entrepreneurship, global economy, forecasting, environment.*

Introduction

A little over 200 years ago, French economist J.B. Say remarked, "The entrepreneur shifts economic resources out of an area of lower into an area of higher productivity and greater yield." The entrepreneur starts his own new and small business, although Drucker noted that not every new small business is entrepreneurial or represents entrepreneurship. Also, not every entrepreneurial business is innovative. Drucker identified entrepreneurs as people who see "change" as the standard, echoing Heraclitus of Ephesus, the Greek philosopher who said, "The only constant in life is change." Entrepreneurs regard change as essential and welcome it as beneficial to the lives of big corporations and small businesses alike. However, the kind of change implied here, Drucker clarified, is typically not the kind that can be brought about simply by deciding to create it. Rather, it is created by entrepreneurs who actively go looking for existing change in order to exploit it. Entrepreneurship is not solely based on purposeful information. Within corporations, those who look for change are considered the trouble makers who often end up starting their own companies. In many cases, they are programmed for inflexibility, leaving employees no longer agile enough to cope with change.

The world has started accepting India as a major player in global economics. Analysts and industry people prophesy India to be a major power of the future. This is still a distant dream because India has a large youth population of 3,000 lakh with just 1,000 lakh jobs to accommodate them. The million dollar question is, which industry has got the nerve to absorb a work-force of this scale. The only rational answer to this problem is entrepreneurship which in itself comes with a new set of challenges.

The discipline of entrepreneurship generally studies the why, when and how of opportunity creation, recognition and utilisation for providing goods and services through the creation of new firms and within existing firms for both profit and non- profit purposes. Not all opportunity creation will necessarily be in the best interest of society. The reward structure of a society can also lead to a destructive allocation of entrepreneurial talent. In the developing countries, the benefits of innovation by entrepreneurs depend on the characteristics of the system of innovation within which they are embedded. The better the system of innovation, the more able a developing country will be to tap into global technology. Knowledge will circulate better within the domestic economy and the economy will embark on the process of technological upgradation more rapidly.

The impact of innovation is important across the countries and institutional contexts. It can play an important role in catch-up and growth in a global economy. The degree to which the entrepreneur will engage in technical innovation and specialisation depends on the size and functioning of the market. Markets can thus be seen as important drivers of growth and development. In the poorest developing countries, markets unfortunately fail to fulfill this role. The developing country markets are often small, fragmented and imperfect due to lack of infrastructure, low per capita incomes, misguided policies and institutional constraints. Political stability, predictability and transparency, peace and other institutional prerequisites for the functioning of markets are often absent. With fragmented, small and uncertain markets there is often insufficient incentive for entrepreneurs to innovate. Hence government support is required for innovation and entrepreneurship in the developing countries.

Conceptual approaches to entrepreneurship

Three main conceptual approaches to entrepreneurship are found in the literature. The first, a functional approach, is concerned with the dynamic actors who make key decisions on investment, production, innovation, location, research and development. From this perspective, entrepreneurship is a psychological trait referring to dynamism, creativity and originality. This approach also includes managers of multi-national firms, state enterprises or non-profit organisations, and a variety of dynamic entrepreneurs within organisations.

The second approach focuses on the firm as the key economic actor. The firms included here are owner operated firms, incorporated joint stock companies, state- owned firms' joint ventures and subsidiaries of multi-nationals. These firms are the units that make the key decisions on investment, on branching into new activities or sectors, or relocating to other countries. The third conceptual approach focuses on owner operated enterprises. Within this approach, the entrepreneur is the person who is both owner and is actively involved in running the business. This relates to mainly small and medium sized enterprises (SMEs), start-ups and self-employment. As stated in the *Oxford Handbook of Innovation,* the concept of innovation refers to the putting into practice of inventions. A narrow, strictly-technological approach focuses specifically on product and process innovations, or technological innovation, which is often said to be the result of technology entrepreneurship. A broader approach refers to innovation as not only the development of new products, new processes and new sources of supply, but also to the exploitation of new markets and the development of new ways to organise business.

Innovative performance has been measured in a variety of ways: using patents, trademarks, R&D inputs and other secondary indicators such as publications or citations. Since the 1980s, increased use has been made of innovation surveys amongst firms. Starting with the European Community Innovation Surveys (CIS), innovation surveys have since spread to the developing world (in particular to Latin America, but also to Asia and southern Africa). In innovation surveys, firms are asked whether they have introduced innovations. The main focus in most innovation surveys is on technological innovations resulting in new products or new production processes.

Innovation and entrepreneurship in India

Globally, India is considered as a country with aversion to innovation and entrepreneurship. The condition aggravates with the fact that we traditionally have invested very small amounts in R&D facilities. In the year 2007-08, we had spent only 0.93 per cent of GNP on R&D, with the lion's share going into strategic (military) development. This can be further substantiated by the fact that on the one hand the R&D expenditure of all Indian industries taken together is less than that of a single Japanese company (Sony) while on the other hand, 12 per cent of the world's total R&D expenditure in 2005 was by China. A comforting fact is that Indians have a tendency of self-employment which was revealed in the 62nd round of NSSO's report on employment, showing a national average of 254 per 1000. A quick glance at history reinforces the belief that even Indians are entrepreneurs. Karsanbhai's Nirma, Munjal's Hero, Iyengar's TVS group, Dhirubhai's Reliance, Kiran Shaw's Biocon, Bharti's Airtel are few examples out of the inexhaustible list of Indians who have carved a niche in the golden temple of fame. The large population in India not only poses huge challenges for the country but at the same time opens the golden door of opportunity. A third of India's population was below 15 years of age in 2000 and close to 20 per cent was in the 15-24 age group. It is expected that in 2020, the average Indian will be only 29 years old, compared with 37 in China and the US and 48 in Japan. This ensures that India in no way can fall short of man-power in the next few decades, and this can sustain India's growth story in the long run.

World over companies are eyeing Indian markets because of high domestic demand and a robust growth supplementing it. This gives an opportunity to entrepreneurs for exploring the latent needs of the Indian customers. The launch of Kinetic scooters at a time when no Indian would have ever imagined a non-steel, self- start, gearless scooter is a case in point. According to a McKinsey report, Indian families are already saving too much to support small businesses directly. Comparing India with South Korea in 2005, both had an almost identical national savings to GDP ratio of about 33 per cent. Yet, in Korea's case, households accounted for just a fifth of the overall rate, compared with 69 per cent in India. The gross domestic savings in the year ending March 31, 2008 were almost 35 per cent of the GDP. That is almost 10 percentage points higher than that of

2003. Add a small amount of capital absorbed through a current account deficit, estimated to be less than 2 per cent of GDP, and India has enough fuel for an economic growth of 8-9 per cent. With more productive use of capital, even 10 per cent is feasible. These savings, under expert guidance and mentorship, can work wonders for aspiring and budding entrepreneurs. India is making headlines due to its partial immunity from the global meltdown. It is true that although there is slowdown in a few sectors, majority of the industries have shown a promising profit which is remarkable. Layoffs and cost cutting are a global phenomenon but India is largely unaffected. A report by Hewitt states that over 60 per cent of the companies are still hiring, and 9 out of 10 companies are still promoting. There is a silver lining to every cloud, is as true as ever.

Globally, Indians are being sent back due to lack of employment opportunities, but the catch is that these Indians are flushed with funds and have valuable experience. This is an ideal mix to start new ventures. There is an abundance of skilled and experienced persons in the market who can be a great asset for any new company. The world "Doing business report 2009", published by World Bank and International Finance Corporation, ranks India 122nd out of 181 countries, whereas even countries like Pakistan stand at 77th. Unless the strong and inseparable link between entrepreneurship and innovation is recognised and acknowledged, entrepreneurship development measures will not have result orientation, and that is the reason for India training so far behind. The sorry story of bureaucracy and red tapism still haunt the Indian businessman. "Single Window Clearance" can act as a booster for novice entrepreneurs. Implementing such process in itself is a herculean task for the government, as this practice has been nurtured by the bureaucrats for decades. However, this is the only way out if we want to progress.

There are more than 5,000 Industrial Training Institutes (ITIs) in India. However, the quality of training is rather uneven, inspite of implementing the upgradation programme. These ITIs produce 7,00,000 technicians each year. Improving their skill levels would be a very powerful channel of advancing India's technical/ manufacturing capabilities. India is unable to compete against countries like China in manufacturing world class products because of shortage of skilled technicians. The institutes have bottlenecks like poor infrastructure, outdated curriculum, less qualified instructors and limited interaction with industry. Skilled labour can be a huge advantage for entrepreneurs to be competitive. These entrepreneurs are generally not in a position to train employees and then use them as it involves a huge cost and is a deterrent for their growth.

We have world class educational institutions such as the IIMs and IITs. There are companies that train their own work-force and if these companies join hands, with government's support and guidance from successful educational institutions, they can reach new acme of success. A small seed today is a big tree tomorrow. Even companies like Infosys, Reliance, Oberoi Hotels had a modest start. It is a well accepted fact that SMEs play a vital role in any country's growth. The contribution of SMEs to GDP in 2003 ranged over 60 per cent in China, 57 per cent in Germany and 55.3 per cent in Japan whereas, as per Assocham's report, India was still slogging around 17 per cent and trying to reach 25 per cent by 2012. Continuous support for technological upgradation, credit availability and export promotion by the government can be a great support. IIMs and IITs have started the concept of incubation, where new companies are promoted within their premises (Silicon Valley similarly promoted by Stanford University). This idea could be implemented on a larger scale along with industry associations. Developing self-help groups (cluster development) by NGOs like SEWA and BASIX has initiated a mass movement of self-employment through micro finance. There are organisations like Shri Mahila Grih Udyog which started off with a borrowed sum of 80 and have a turnover of ₹ 470 crore, which includes ₹ 24 crore of exports. This showcases the potential of entrepreneurs.

Innovation on a global scale

Innovation as a practice has come a long way since Drucker shared his ideas in the 1980s.For starters, any present day discussion about innovation is likely to include references to international initiatives. Also, due to the global economy, measuring innovative performance has moved to the top of corporate executives' agendas. In fact, global innovation now has a formal means of measurement. The Global Innovative Index (GII), conceived and developed by INSEAD Business School and World Business, is a formal model built to better see which nations are currently meeting the challenges of innovation. The GII ranks the world's best and worst performing economies from the standpoint of innovation, as well as providing insights into nations' strengths and weaknesses in their innovation-related policies and practices. The availability of this Index means business leaders can more assuredly make revealing comparisons and critical decisions because their research is based on concrete data. Since the GII shows to what degree individual nations and regions currently respond to the challenge of innovation, it will begin to paint a picture of what constitutes success and what does not. Along the same lines, many questions are being asked about measuring entrepreneurship.

There are countries that have enormous success with innovation, yet they often have trouble getting these products to market. To get actionable information, we need to look at entrepreneurship and innovation interchangeably and develop an index to reveal the linkage between them on a global basis.

Global innovation and entrepreneurship: future forecast

Based on the current information available, innovation and entrepreneurship will continue to expand in future across the borders, because of the existence of these six circumstances: global market conditions, entrepreneurial mindset, eroding confidence in established institutions, shifting business environment, international collaboration and environmental/technological advancements.

1. Global market conditions

Trade barriers are easing. Economies are becoming inter-dependent. Communication via the Internet has never been easier or more accessible. These conditions drive political reform, cultural transparency, social progress and a great deal of wealth creation.

2. Entrepreneurial mindset

Entrepreneurs have the ability to see, understand and take advantage of evolving markets. The ability to think differently, use insights, see what others do not, envision what does not yet exist, and identify the opportunity when it is ripe are the prized qualities of today's entrepreneur.

3. Eroding confidence in established institutions

The recent world economic meltdown is removing any last confidence that most people had in governments, large enterprises, banks and other financial entities. The resulting mistrust will lead to reinventing ourselves as individuals, communities, countries and societies. As such, many more entrepreneurs will be joining the field.

4. Shifting business environment

Large scale firms are synonymous with bureaucracy which tends to stifle innovation. In response, the business environment is shifting to accommodate the needs of its rapidly changing market players. Innovation and entrepreneurship are beginning to flourish around the world and will likely take the form of much smaller, yet bolder companies. Knowing and catering to it is how entrepreneurial ventures beat corporate giants to the punch. Any company, large or small, that continues down the same path it has always taken will find it to be a losing proposition.

5. Entrepreneurial collaboration

Also, on a global scale, there will be more entrepreneurial collaboration, which in turn will make shared innovation between countries a far more common occurrence at the company-to-company level, not just at universities and research institutions. One of China's approaches for creating an innovative nation is the Technology Business Incubator (TBI). China's mission is to nurture "technopreneurs" and technology based start-ups. Business incubation is considered a viable option for countries that want to expand economic opportunities.

6. Growth of environmental and sustainable engineering technologies

A growing consciousness about the value of protecting our world will fuel the demand for products and services that can accomplish this goal. In Drucker's words, in the past couple of decades, there has been an exodus of people to words "West" for good education and they often ended up staying back because of the rich opportunities that existed. But now, these opportunities are not limited to the West. Opportunities are international in scope, and people are choosing to return to their homeland to utilise their newly acquired talent and to build fortunes with it, and elevate global competition. The demand for innovation on an international scale and for the entrepreneurship that accompanies it will focus increasingly on being more purpose driven.

Conclusion

It is apparent that India has a long way to go before making a mark on the world map as a developed and prosperous nation. The dream can be realised by improving the quality of life of its masses which can only be done by generating employment for them. The seemingly insatiable demand for jobs can only be met by promoting entrepreneurial activities by giving the right platform to entrepreneurs with the help of organisations such as NEN and The Indus Entrepreneurs. It is pretty evident that Indians have launched new ventures with flair in the past and they still possess the fire. Opportunities are in abundance and the country is plush with resources. The formidable challenge lies in optimising the resources and overcoming the hurdles to not only joining the league of successful and developed nations but rather setting an example for other developing nations. The impact of innovation is important across the countries and institutional contexts. It can play an important role in catch-up and growth in a global economy. Most of these entrepreneurs work within SMEs where the extent of their innovativeness depends on the characteristics of the entrepreneur (education, age, experience, networks), as well as the region (location) and the sector (technological intensity) in which the firm is active. There is no shortage of entrepreneurship in the developing countries. But the policy and institutional environment are an important determinant of innovative behaviour. Government support for innovation are important. This can take many forms ranging from reform of the environment for doing business to providing venture capital, tapping into migrant workers and provision of technical and managerial education, infrastructure and more active state-private sector partnerships. Sometimes, even an adverse environment can spur innovative behaviour and entrepreneurs may become the drivers of policy and institutional change, rather than only being determined by the policy and institutional environment. With intention at the helm, innovation and entrepreneurship will adapt to accommodate the changing focus of the drive to live a better life, do good, save the planet and make money.

8

What Motivates the Entrepreneur: Personal or Social Gain?

– *Brajaballav Kar*
Sushree Ranjan Tripathy

Abstract

There are many motives for choosing entrepreneurship as career. Literature indicates wealth motives and independence as most important drivers of intention. Social entrepreneurship as a career choice has social well being as a distinct driver of motivation. In one direction the entrepreneur is aggrandising wealth for self and in the other the entrepreneur is sacrificing for the common good. The research investigates this dichotomy among existing entrepreneurs and finds the dominant intention paradigm. The research design takes the convenient sampling of 213 entrepreneurs and seeks the response on a 5-point Likert scale. The data analysis indicates that entrepreneurship intent has a strong social dimension and entrepreneurs think creation of social well being is one of the prime motivations. It indicates that addressing social problems and creation of social benefit are the roles entrepreneurs take up. It also indicates that the employees of the organisation, community and other social institutions tend to gain from the entrepreneurial process. The research suggests that the community also needs to reciprocate by supporting the entrepreneurial effort.

Introduction

Entrepreneurs are the change agents and their contribution to the socio-economic development is immense. Specifically their role becomes important in developing countries. They are alert to economic opportunities and try to exploit such opportunities for gain. Entrepreneurship involves substantial risk. It involves searching for economically exploitable ideas, investing hard earned savings and investing substantial time. It is not whimsical behaviour, it is planned. However, it is also seen that such entrepreneurial endeavour is not always because of the desire for self-aggrandisement, it can be due to an intense desire to do good for the society. Doing good may not result in wealth accumulation for the entrepreneur individually, it may give a sense of satisfaction. Are these entrepreneurial objectives dichotomous? Could it indicate that these seemingly dichotomous intentions are coterminous? This research tries to investigate these factors through existing entrepreneurs in the socio-economic context of Odisha, India

Literature review

Literature indicates many motives for entrepreneurship (Kar et al. 2014). Entrepreneurship is the only career where entrepreneurs are directly responsible for multiple stake-holders. Entrepreneurs gain economic advantage by having product or service knowledge, understanding of the competitors, customers, suppliers; own employees as well as, by an uncanny ability, to foresee the future. The entrepreneur manages multiple and contradictory objectives in any business, sets priorities and becomes the embodiment of different functions, processes and policies of the new venture. Very few of the entrepreneurial efforts become successful, indicating a very high level of risk.The question remains as to why do individuals attempt entrepreneurship.

Many a time the entrepreneur is also classified as an opportunist (Kirzner 1973; Eckhardt and Shane 2003), capitalist (Formaini 2001) and profit seeking individual (McDaniel 2005) with scant regard to the benefits of the stake-holders. The dominant motive is attributed to self-aggrandisement. They exploit the opportunity by finding loopholes in the law, taking advantage of the vulnerable employees, customers and using the information asymmetry. In a perfectly competitive economy and egalitarian society entrepreneur is a criminal or at least an anathema, yet the society craves for them in the name of growth and development.

But many times it is the entrepreneur who is responsible for bringing innovations to use, help the society and economy grow (Kirton 1976; Cefis and Marsili 2006). The actions of the entrepreneurs question the status quo of the society and economy. Innovations, better products and services, cost-effective solutions are the greatest contributions for the mankind. Their action reduces the disparity between the haves and have-not, different locations, etc. They bring new socio-economic order (Schumpeter 1911) into the world. The society pays the dividend to entrepreneurs in the form of wealth; the significant risk is also associated with its own awards.

The entrepreneurial risk taking and innovation have an inevitable social dimension in that the offerings of entrepreneurship are for the society only. Creation of a new venture has also the ethical dimension of caring for the employees, customers and well being of the society. Entrepreneurial ethics is of utmost importance since it forms the base, the common and shared value system around which the organisation and the larger community interacts (Longenecker et al. 1989; Hannafey 2003). Lack of ethics jeopardises the sustainability of the organisation. The value proposition of a newfirm in itself ensures the well being of all. At the very base level, the well being can be construed as the market need. The larger the number of stake-holders and wider the solution proposition the longer is the sustainability of the organisation. So the well being as a philosophy has to be in-built into the business proposition. Established businesses have embraced corporate social responsibility, which indicates that the commercial profit orientation and philanthropy have been co-terminating. Some research also indicated entrepreneurs to have a spirit of sacrifice.

Culture has deep impact on formation of entrepreneurship (Hayton, George & Zahra 2002). To an extent, protestant ethos also has been indicated to be a cultural element promoting entrepreneurship. Many cultures where resources are scarce have become entrepreneurial rather than where there is abundance of resources. People of such cultures practice frugality, postponement of gratification and compulsive savings. They also are religious about benevolence and gratitude as a principle of life. Thus the cultural elements form the DNA of entrepreneurship. There has been a great deal of criticism about the cultural and philosophical practices in India and the Hindu religion being the reason for lack of entrepreneurial culture. Wealth making is taken to be a less important work and looked down upon. Spiritual attainment is the highest ideal for people. The religion also promotes individual excellence as opposed to group attainment. The idea of being born alone and die alone, gives too much importance to individualism. Other message such as "Vasudhaiva Kutumbakam" (world as a family) get lost amidst the plethora of messages promoting individualism. As a religious philosophy the present life is considered transient and illusory. Shunning desires to attain salvation hits most common people to make them disenchanted about entrepreneurial process. The problem gets compounded by the rigmarole of laws, legal shylocks and parasitic bureaucracy. The direct or vicarious experience is tragic enough for a nascent entrepreneur to attempt a Sisyphus-journey. The paradox is that those who are brave or lucky enough to be successful are derided and despised of some means and ends which are not respectable enough. It becomes difficult for people to accept or adore entrepreneurial success. Entrepreneurial failure is compounded with social exclusion along with personal losses. The exit from entrepreneurial career is extremely difficult, organisational acceptance is the least, and Indian employment scenario discriminates failed entrepreneur. Where is the motivation then to be one? Entrepreneurs become social and cultural orphans without legitimacy.

Umpteen entrepreneurs fail umpteen times. Failure is the price the society has to pay to advance. It has to be embraced and encouraged. Unfortunately, it would be political, economical and in principle nightmare to encourage failures. In many cases entrepreneurship is promoted, stage-managed and catapulted to success till it is known to have unholy, illegal nexus of law makers and executives. These kinds of entrepreneurs have undue advantage over factors of production or information; success is attributed to them like a foregone conclusion. Entrepreneurship as a means to hedonistic pleasure early in life becomes an explosive tenet. Such cases spread wrong message regarding the basic tenet of entrepreneurship.

The arguments presented above can be classified broadly into two schools of debate. Whether the intention of entrepreneurship is driven by personal gain or social gain as the predominant motive? Wealth as an outcome of entrepreneurship could be the motive or social good as a process of entrepreneurship could also become the entrepreneurial motive. This research investigates this dichotomy from the responses of existing entrepreneurs.

Methodology

In light of the above discussion the research paper presents the survey results from 213 entrepreneurs of Odisha with regard to motivation of becoming an entrepreneur. Convenient sampling was used for the collection of data. The paper only presents part of a larger study and takes up two motives like "To be rich" and "To create social well being". The larger section of the intention had 20 items and its reliability and validity was checked with Cronbach alpha test of reliability (0.662) and pilot testing of the questionnaire. The questions were to be responded on a five-point Likert scale.

SPSS was used for data analysis. Cross tabulation of the data and frequency plot was taken up to understand the data distribution. Chi-square test was conducted to identify any relationship and subsequently correlation test was done to find the degree and direction of relationship between the two motives as indicated earlier.

Profile of the sample

In the sample of the respondents 75 per cent were males and 25 per cent females. Eighty-three per cent of the total sample were married whereas 17 per cent were unmarried. The age group was distributed as follows: below 25 years of age-4 per cent, between 25 and 35 years-31 per cent, between 35 to 45 years 45 per cent, between 45 to 60 years 16 per cent and more than 60 years 4 per cent of the entrepreneurs. The prior experience profile indicated that in the selected sample 55 per cent had some prior experience before getting into entrepreneurship where as 45 per cent had no prior experience, there was 1 non response for this question.

Data analysis and findings

A. I wanted to become rich by doing business

The questionnaire sought responses to the above statement on a five-point Likert scale. This question was taken from the existing literature about wealth creation being one of the predominant motives of entrepreneurs. Figure-1 indicates the distribution of responses to the question that the entrepreneurs wanted to become rich by doing business.

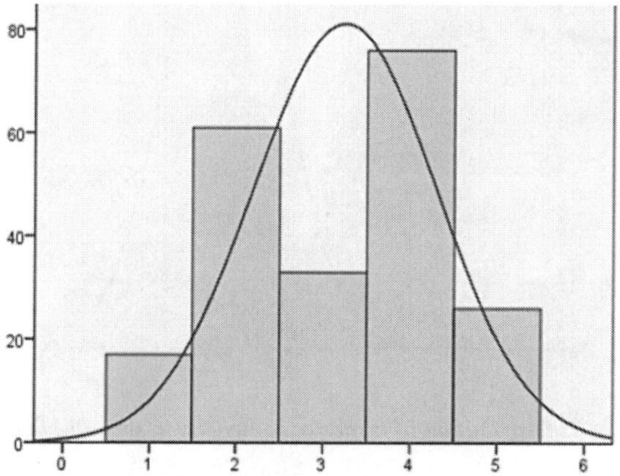

Fig. 8.1: Frequency distribution of responses

The mean of the response was 3.15 on the 5-point Likert scale and the standard deviation was 1.197. In the selected sample as many as 36.6 per cent of the respondents disagree (Strongly 8% and disagree 28.6%) that they wanted to become rich by doing business; on the other hand 47.9 per cent agreed (Strongly agree 12.2% and Agree 35.7%). Importantly, 15.5 per cent of the respondents remained ambivalent about it. The modal value was 4. If the neutral response (Neither agree nor disagree) is not considered, then of the total response 57 per cent agree that they somewhat wanted to become rich by doing business.

B. I wanted to contribute to the social wellbeing

Of the different motives, contribution to social well being is recognised in the literature. Social entrepreneurship as a form is not focused towards personal wealth making; on the contrary it is initiated by the motive to do good for the society. Here the entrepreneur sacrifices for the society rather than gain from the process. One could argue about the nature of gain, but the gain is not in the form of wealth. The five-point Likert scale used from 1-as strongly disagree, up to 5-as strongly agree, with 3 as the neutral value. The distribution of the responses is presented below.

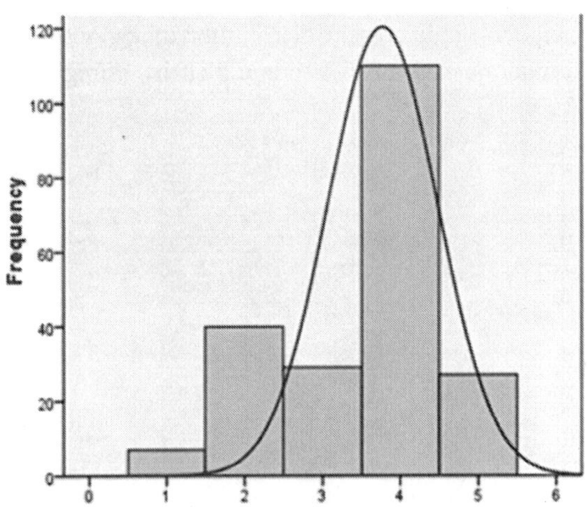

Fig. 8.2: Distribution of response contribute to social wellbeing

The data indicates that the response to this question has a mean of 3.52 and standard deviation of 1.04. 64.3 per cent agree (agree 51.6 % and Strongly agree 12.7 %) with the proposition whereas only 22.1 per cent disagree (Strongly disagree 3.3 % and Disagree 18.8 %). If the neutral response (Neither agree nor Disagree) is not considered, then of the total responses 75 per cent agree that there was a motive for business, to contribute to the social well being.

Cross tabulation

The cross tabulation of the responses is shown below. Thirty seven percent disagree that to be rich was the motive compared to 22 per cent disagree about social well being. Sixty-four per cent agree to social well being as the predominant motive as compared to 48 per cent to make wealth.

Table - 8.1: Social well being vs to be rich

		Social well being			*Total*
		Disagree	*Neutral*	*Agree*	
To be rich	Disagree	9 (4%)	4 (2%)	65 (31%)	78 (37%)
	Neutral	11 (5%)	5 (2%)	17 (8%)	33 (15%)
	Agree	27 (13%)	20 (9%)	55 (26%)	102 (48%)
Total		**47 (22%)**	**29 (14%)**	**137 (64%)**	**213 (100%)**

Chi square test of relationship was conducted to understand if there exists some relationship between the two variables of business intention. The chi square test of relationship indicates (chi square= 20.527, Df=4, Significance=0.000) that there is a relationship between variables "to be rich" and "social well being" as motive to do business and the relationship is significant.

The correlation between the two variables was tested and it was found that (Pearson's r= -.237, significance = .000) there is negative coefficient of correlation between the two variables, which is significant. These two motivational factors are directionally opposite to each other.

Discussion and conclusion

The data analysis indicates that "social well being" is a more predominant motive as compared to "to be rich". It may be argued that social well being is concomitant with become rich; however, this research indicates that the relationship is negative. Thus social well being is a distinctive motive for entrepreneurship. Possibly, the entrepreneur gets a greater meaning and purpose in social well being. In a sense, entrepreneurs are willing to take risk for the well being of others. It also indicates that social entrepreneurship would be a preferable mode as compared to business ventures. At the same time social well being has to happen along with the sustenance of business in the long term.

Though it is indicated that social well being is a predominant motive, it is necessary to establish the context and stage at which such intentionality develops. Similarly, the social expectancy bias in the responses also could not be ruled out.

The implication of the finding is significant in the Indian context. There has to be a shift of perception among the common public towards entrepreneurs. Entrepreneurs strive for the betterment of society instead of their own personal goal. Thus it is a societal onus to facilitate entrepreneurship in every possible way, starting from the formation of intent till the successful and sustainable operation.

Limitations and scope for further research

The existing research has taken convenient samples and thus the findings could not be generalized. A larger and probabilistic sampling plan would indicate more robust finding. Similarly the research finding could vary across different sections of the sample which could be investigated in future research.

9

Fostering Entrepreneurship, Innovation, Inclusiveness: Start-up and Stand-up

– D. Nagayya

Balla Appa Rao

"I see start-ups, technology and innovation as exciting and effective instruments for India's transformation".

Narendra Modi, Prime Minister of India

Abstract

The article focuses on new directions and strategies of entrepreneurship, innovation and inclusiveness through two programmes launched by the Union governement in January 2016, for which the Department of Industrial Policy and Promotion (DIPP) is the nodal agency. They are Start- up India and Stand-up India initiatives. Start-up India, as outlined in the Action Plan, refers to promotion of innovative enterprises with considerable extent of research and development carried out in collaboration with higher educational and scientific research institutions. Technology Business Incubators promoted for this purpose are normally established in collaboration with a host of leading higher educational and scientific research institutions. Linking industry with academia to focus on new areas that have potential for development is the direction planned to be pursued for encouraging start- up entities in various sectors. The entities are sector and scale neutral. To facilitate the youth to take up innovative ventures, creating a favourable and liberal eco system is a pre-requisite. Easier entry and faster exit are emphasised for the success of these enterprises which involve high risk. The article presents opportunities and challenges along with strategies. In this programme, the key players that deserve special mention are Department of Science and Technology (DST) and Department of Industrial Policy and Promotion of the Government of India, and Small Industries Development Bank of India (SIDBI) among development financial institutions. Stand-up India programme refers to promotion of micro, small and medium enterprises (MSMEs) by women and SC/ST entrepreneurs across the country with focus on rural and semi-urban areas, and remote and less developed regions. This speaks of inclusiveness. Entrepreneurs promoting MSMEs can pursue these high potential directions which are prone to high risk and yield high reward.

Keywords: *Start-up, stand-up, innovation, entrepreneurship, incubator*

Introduction

India has been progressively moving towards an economy driven by knowledge and innovation. The *Global Competitiveness Report (GCR)*, released annually by the World Economic Forum (WEF), Davos (Switzerland) classifies national economies into three broad categories: (a) factor-driven, (b) efficiency-driven, and (c) innovation-driven. Many economies are considered to be in the transitional phase between any two given broad groups. These categories are seen as indicators of a development ladder. In factor-driven economies, economic development is primarily driven by basic requirements of various sectors. In efficiency-driven economies, government's focus is on ensuring the smooth functioning of mechanisms such as markets and technological progress. In the innovation-driven economies, entrepreneurial framework conditions become more important as levers of economic development than basic requirements and efficiency enhancers. The outcome of the model is national economic growth through, for example, job creation and technical innovation.

In the Global Competitiveness Index (GCI) 2016 as published in GCR 2016, India has scored 16 points, rising to 39th position from the 55th by rising rapidly among all countries. In GCR 2015 also it was stated that India has scored 16 points and moved up from its earlier ranking of 71 to 55, out of a total of 144 countries. Among the emerging and developing Asian nations, India ranks sixth after Malaysia (18), China (28), Thailand (32), Indonesia (37), and the Philippines (47). India has the potential to move ahead of these countries. Despite moving 15 places up to 66th rank from the 81st in the Global Innovation Index (GII) as published in GCR 2015, India has a long way to go in promoting innovation, and scientific and industrial research. In the World Bank's Ease of Doing Business Ranking 2015, India is placed at 142 out of a total of 189 economies. But on the start-up front, India ranks third globally with 4,200 start- up entities, next only to USA and UK. The new initiatives in promoting start-ups would enable India to progress fast.

The *Global Entrepreneurship Monitor (GEM)*, released annually from USA, has focused on entrepreneurship as a process comprising different phases, namely, from intending to start, to just starting, to operating new or established enterprises, and even discontinuing the business. GEM 2014 describes India as an emerging entrepreneurial country, giving details as follows: In India, 4.1 per cent of adults are 'nascent entrepreneurs' (actively involved in setting up a business), while 2.5 per cent are 'new business owners' (in operation for more than 3 but less than 42 months). Combining these two stages gives us the Total early stage Entrepreneurial Activity (TEA) rate, meaning that close to 7 per cent of the Indian adult population, or 1 in every 15 adults, are engaged in some form of early stage entrepreneurial activity. In India, adults are generally positive about entrepreneurship. GEM 2014 showed that 58 per cent of Indian adults (aged between 18 and 64 years) considered entrepreneurship as a desirable career choice; and around 66 per cent of adults thought that entrepreneurs received a high status and respect in the society (*India MSME Report* 2015: 72).

Start-up India: An initiative for innovation and inclusiveness

Among the turnaround initiatives introduced in the past two years by the Union government, special mention may be made of Start-up India and Stand-up India to promote entrepreneurship, innovation and inclusive development at all levels of economic growth and social development process. Start-up India is a flagship initiative of the Government of India, intended to build a strong eco system for nurturing innovation. This will drive sustainable economic growth and generate large scale employment opportunities. It is the platform where creative and innovative youth will get a forum to translate their dream into reality. The youth of India today have the confidence to venture out on their businesses and enterprises through innovative approaches. Therefore, a favourable and liberal eco system is a pre- requisite to helping them succeed. The following paragraphs discuss Start-up India features first, and then Stand-up India in the second half of the article.

Start-up is an expression generally used in the MSME sector to refer to entrepreneurs who have promoted enterprises recently or prospective entrepreneurs about to launch the enterprises. In this sector, technocrat entrepreneurs who have expertise in certain product lines, keen on promoting new enterprises are given encouragement and hand-holding support through a number of incentives and facilities. This category is given special recognition through science and technology oriented entrepreneurship development programmes. One of the attributes of this group is to take up enterprises for which processes have been developed but have not yet been commercially proved successful, i.e., those product lines/processes with high risk and high reward. Special institutional infrastructure and programme content have been developed for this group of entrepreneurs. Science and Technology Entrepreneurs Parks (STEPs), Software Technology Parks (STPs), and Technology Business Incubators (TBIs) have been developed in different regions to meet their needs. In the newly announced Start-up India initiative, launched on 16th January 2016 by the Prime Minister through a Start-up Action Plan, the term is given special connotation, as presented in this section, specifically applicable for innovative enterprises where innovativeness is identified and certified by a government recognised organisation such as an incubator. The entity is sector and scale neutral, and can be in any of the sectors such as agriculture, manufacturing, health care, education and other social sectors, bio-technology, information technology, IT-linked activities, consumer electronics, etc. Emphasis is on IT and IT-related services to begin with, with the intention of promoting scale neutral entities, and encourage not only youth from within the country, but also attract non-resident Indians and experienced persons from other countries to participate in the 'Make in India' campaign. Two other criteria to be fulfilled are: (a) the enterprise registered not earlier than five years, and (b) annual turnover in the recent five years not exceeding ₹ 25 crore. The nodal agency for the start-up policy is the Department of Industrial Policy and Promotion of the Union Ministry of Commerce and Industry. In terms of scale of operation, entrepreneurs in the MSME sector can also participate, provided they are able to fulfill various conditions and attributes that go with the definition of a start-up entity in the present Start-up India initiative. For MSME entrepreneurs not able to come up to the criteria laid down for the newly announced start-up programme in the Start-up Action Plan formulated by the DIPP, MSME promotion package relevant to their needs can be considered by them for establishing the enterprise of their choice.

Definition of Start-up India

Start-up means an entity incorporated or registered in India not prior to five years, with annual turnover not exceeding ₹ 25 crore in any preceding financial year, working towards innovation, development, deployment or commercialisation of new products, processes or services driven by technology or intellectual property,

(a) provided that such entity is not formed by splitting up or reconstruction of a business already in existence;

(b) provided also that an entity shall cease to be a start-up if its turnover for the previous financial years has exceeded ₹ 25 crore or it has completed 5 years from the date of incorporation or registration.

(c) A start-up shall be eligible for tax benefits only after it is certified by an inter- ministerial board. For this purpose, the start-up should be supported by a recommendation, with regard to innovative nature of business from a government recognised incubator.

(d) The mere act of developing products or services that do not have the potential for commercialisation or undifferentiated products or services or processes, or have no or limited incremental value for customers would not be a start-up. Smaller ventures would seek funding on their own, and without official sops, but the government must not lose sight of the need to fix India's overall business climate." [DIPP (2016), Start-up Action Plan, New Delhi].

Process of setting up a start-up entity

Start-ups can be identified as enterprises with innovative ideas, often in the areas of emerging technologies, launched by technically qualified entrepreneurs. The start-up entrepreneurs are qualified in their respective areas of specialisation. The enterprises are launched to develop business models based on innovative ideas of the entrepreneurs. While the growth rate of the successful start-ups is very high, many of which reach the corporate status within a couple of years, the failure rate of the starters has also been observed to be very high, even at the global level.

Many of such enterprises start at the 'micro' level, with a number of them either in the area of Information and Communication Technologies or predominantly leaning on IT based tools in their business. Again the global experience reveals that the start-ups are located in and around premier technical insttitutions to avail of the expertise of the mother institution while developing the business model. The 'Silicon Valley' experience is the global benchmark for promoting and supporting the start-ups. Another direction for identifying innovative ideas for start-ups is to collaborate with the network of national laboratories of the Council of Scientific and Industrial Research (CSIR) to take up unproven technologies or processes, or those which have been tried out only in a few locations in the country. These refer to high risk and high reward technologies. A third direction is linkage with the major industrial enterprises such as medium, large and mega projects in the country for identifying the project ideas. Yet another direction is to tie up with projects in other countries in areas of interest to the entrepreneurs. These approaches do not rule out the scope for micro and small enterprises to experiment with innovative ideas. The entrepreneurs need to explore the scope for these enterprises to exploit the latent potential. Towards protecting the intellectual properties (IP) generated by the start-up, the Government assists in filing of patents or alternative IP protection mechanisms. The IP facilitation centres set up under the IPR component of the National Manufacturing Competitiveness Programme (NMCP) may be the nodal points in guiding, hand- holding, and subsidising the start-up entrepreneurs in protecting their IPRs.

Latest policy initiatives for innovative start-up entities

To simplify the regulatory framework, the government introduced the Ease of Doing Business wherein an MSME unit has to fill in a single one page self-declaration online form called Udyog Aadhaar. This single page memorandum constitutes a self- declaration under which the MSME will certify its existence and areas of operation, promoter/owner Aadhaar details, bank account details, and other basic minimum information. With the single window clearance mechanism in operation at various levels, the effort is to create a business friendly environment with easy entry and easy exit procedures to encourage entrepreneurial activity. Under the Apprentice Protsahan Yojana, 50 per cent of stipend payable to the apprentices would be reimbursed by the Government for the first two years, which is an incentive for MSME units to take more apprentices.

To give boost to the Make in India programme, the Union MSME Ministry has launched the ASPIRE scheme in March 2015. ASPIRE is the abbreviation of the scheme for promotion of Innovation, Entrepreneurship, and Agro industry. It has the objectives of creating new jobs to reduce unemployment, promoting entrepreneurship culture across regions in the country, achieving rural industrialisation in less developed regions as well, and promoting innovative business solutions, thus strengthening the competitiveness of enterprises. The scheme provides a framework for promotion of start-up enterprises in agro and rural industries through forward and backward linkages. Setting up of business incubators and technology business centres, and guiding entrepreneurs from selection of project ideas to implementation of the project are all covered at different stages under this scheme (www.msme.org).

Atal Innovation Mission (AIM)

AIM and Atal Incubation Centre (AIC), operated by NITI Aayog, are about innovation promotion platform involving academics, entrepreneurs and researchers, and draw upon national and international experiences to foster a culture of innovation, R & D, and scientific research in India. The platform will promote a network of world class innovation hubs and grand challenges for India. SETU (Self-Employment and Talent Utilisation) is a techno-financial, incubation and facilitation programme to support all aspects of start-up businesses and other self-employment activities. The objectives of AIM and SETU are to serve as a platform for promotion of innovation hubs, start-up businesses, and self-employment activities particularly in technology-driven areas. For AIM and SETU, Government has announced an initial sum of ₹ 500 crore and ₹ 1,000 crore, respectively. AIM is a mission, and SETU is an approach. Therefore, it is considered desirable to have one umbrella scheme, titled AIM, which covers two sub-components: (a) innovation, and (b) SETU, wherein the innovators would be supported and mentored as successful entrepreneurs. The overall purpose of the AIM is to promote a culture of entrepreneurship and innovation in the country. The key objectives of the AIM include the following:

- To create an umbrella structure to oversee innovation eco system of the country;
- To provide a platform and collaboration opportunities for different stakeholders;
- To develop new programmes and policies for fostering innovation in different sectors of the economy; and
- To create awareness, and provide knowledge inputs in creating innovation challenges, and funding mechanism to the government.

Already applications have been invited to establish laboratories and incubation centres for this purpose. Under the scheme, each AIC will be eligible to a grant-in-aid of ₹ 10 crore per annum for a maximum of 5 years, towards the capital and operational expenditure in running the centre. To qualify for the support, the applicant has to provide a built-up space of at least 10,000 sq.ft.

Electronics Development Fund (EDF)

The Ministry of Communications and Information Technology (C&IT) has created the Electronics Development Fund to promote innovation, research and development, and product development in the field of semi-conductors, nanoelectronics, IT and associated sectors by bringing in established companies and start-ups on board. For accelerating research, design and development of electronic products within the country, start-up units would be provided supportive financial assistance from the EDF. A few other ministries of the GoI have created similar funds for the benefit of start-ups in product lines coming under their purview. These include Departments of Bio-technology, and Electronics and Information Technology.

India Aspiration Fund (IAF) and SMILE of SIDBI

With ₹ 2,000 crore corpus India Aspiration Fund was launched by SIDBI in August 2015 to boost start-ups, fund-of-funds eco system. This fund would invest in various venture capital funds for meeting the equity requirement of MSME start-ups. A SIDBI Make in India Loan for Small Enterprises (SMILE) scheme of ₹ 10,000 crore has also been launched to catalyse tens of thousands of crore of equity investment in start-ups and MSMEs, creating employment opportunities mostly for educated youth over the next few years. The objective of SMILE is to provide loans in the nature of quasi-equity and term loans on relatively soft terms to MSMEs to meet the required debt-equity ratio norm. The 25 sectors under the Make in India programme would be the focus with emphasis on financing of smaller enterprises in the MSME sector. Concessional terms will be applicable for enterprises promoted by women, SC/ST/persons with disabilities.

Till date start-ups have been successful in e-commerce and other IT based applications of the services sector. The start-ups in the manufacturing sector are yet to take off in a big way.

The Union government is committed towards providing an environment for start- ups to thrive in, as India is at the fore-front of an entrepreneurial revolution, Union Commerce and Industry Minister Nirmala Sitharaman stated, speaking at the Start-up India States' Conference in New Delhi on 23rd July 2016. Highlighting the government's efforts to improve ease of doing business, she said, a start-up would now require only a certificate of recognition from the DIPP for IPR related benefits. A panel of facilitators has also been constituted to provide assistance in the process, wherein DIPP would bear the facilitation cost.

"In order to avail IPR-related benefits - rebate in fee up to 80 per cent, and free of cost facilitation of filing IPR applications - a start-up will now be required to obtain only a certificate of recognition from DIPP, and will not be required to be examined by the Inter-Ministerial Board, as was being done till recently, the minister stated. DIPP has also written to top 50 companies requesting them to support Start-up India initiative under CSR (Corporate Social Responsibility) activities by setting up new incubators in collaboration with educational institutions. Reacting to the success of start-ups, the minister observed that start-up rate of success, world over, is not very high. But that is the nature of business. What the government can do is to give a chance for every idea to reach some stage which otherwise would not have materialised. Given the tax breaks, it becomes easier for start-ups to get funds. The market will determine which ideas should go commercial. India has been pegged at the third place behind the US and UK in terms of number of start-ups: 4,200 technology start-ups exist in India at present, and the number is expected to reach over 12,000 by 2020 (*The Hindu*, Vijayawada edition, July 24, 2016).

The response to the start-up policy has been lukewarm up to end June 2016: the DIPP received 571 applications. Of these, 106 had the required documents. DIPP said only 12 applicants could be considered for tax benefits as these were started after 1st April 2016. Among them, seven applicants had furnished all the required documents. The remaining applicants would be given guidance and support by the Start-up India Hub.

Funding pattern for start-ups

For financing start-up enterprises, conventional banking facilities can be of help at a later stage of development of the enterprise, after it settles down as a moderately successful unit. In the early stage, beginning from conceiving innovative ideas and trying them on an experimental basis, world over angel funds and subsequently venture capitalists provide capital support. When the business model reaches the stage of commercial success, the growth rate of the start-ups becomes phenomenal, and the enterprises shift to full-fledged industrial premises/offices/laboratories for scaling up the activities with the conventional sources of finance like bank credit. Venture capital funds of SIDBI, and a number of other venture capital companies in the public and private sectors participate in the funding and management of the enterprises. Initial pattern of funding is through equity participation and development loan, and contribution from the government through incentives and tax concessions offered for enterprises fulfilling certain criteria. While the angel and venture capital funds finance a project on the basis of their own risk analysis and valuation, the Government can extend support towards reducing the risk. This could be in the form of a guarantee or co-investment through a government promoted venture fund, in addition to providing a wide range of concessions and incentives.

Institutional infrastructure for start-ups

Regarding infrastructure needed for promoting start-ups, the initial effort at encouraging, mentoring and landholding of start-ups can be through incubators promoted at a host educational institution or a research and scientific body. The incubator hub can provide the necessary facilities in collaboration with the host institution. As the enterprises need to move to their regular industrial premises a few years later, it is important to develop modular industrial estates/laboratories suited to the nature of enterprises to be promoted in that area, with the required plug and play facilities. Linking the enterprises with technical institutions/research bodies on one side and funding agencies on the other is an important direction to be pursued by the incubator hub with the good offices of the key organisations associated with the development of a cluster of enterprises in each location. In the manufacturing activities, the organisational network available in the country beginning from the Development Commissioner (MSME), the SIDBI, and the Export-Import Bank of India (EXIM Bank) can provide the necessary institutional support. Infrastructure can be planned by the state level Infrastructure Development Corporation. As the needs of different groups of start-ups are likely to be different, the requirements of different entities need to be carefully examined for planning the facilities. For coordinating and monitoring the implementation of key areas of the programmes, a Start-up Cell has been created in the office of the Development Commissioner (MSME). The focus is on ensuring the functioning of a single window for the start-ups at various levels. Similarly, in various Ministries / Departments, where clusters of enterprises are being promoted in the disciplines falling under their purview, guardianship is to be ensured through a core team associated with the start-ups programme to provide sustained support at various stages of development of enterprises.

Tax incentives for start-ups in the Union Budget 2016-17

Tax incentives announced for start-ups in the Union Budget 2016-17, and approved by the Parliament are presented here.

(i) A deduction will be made of one hundred per cent of profits and gains derived by an eligible start-up from a business involving innovation, development, deployment or commercialisation of new products, processes or services driven by technology or intellectual property. This benefit shall be available to an eligible start-up which is set up after 1st April 2016 up to end April 2019. Income tax exemption is for three years in a block of five years.

(ii) A new section 54 EE will be inserted to provide exemption from capital gains tax if the long term capital gains proceeds are invested by an assessee in units of such specified fund, as may be notified by the Central Government in this behalf, subject to the condition that the amount remains invested for three years, failing which the exemption shall be withdrawn. The investment in the units of the specified fund shall be allowed up to ₹ 50 lakh.

(iii) The existing provisions of section 54 GB provide exemption from tax on long term capital gains in respect of the gains arising on account of transfer of a residential property, if such capital gains are invested in subscription of shares of a company which qualifies to be a small or medium enterprise under MSME Development Act 2006, subject to other conditions specified therein.

(iv) With a view to providing relief to an individual or HUF willing to set up a start-up company by selling a residential property to invest in the shares of such company, it is proposed to amend section 54 GB so as to provide that long term capital gains arising on account of transfer of residential property shall not be charged to tax if such capital gains are invested in subscription of shares of a company which qualifies to be an eligible start-up subject to the condition that the individual or HUF holds more than fifty per cent shares of the company, and such company utilises the amount invested in shares to purchase new asset before due date of filing of return by the investor. The existing provision of section 54 GB requires that the company should invest the proceeds in the purchase of new asset being new plant and machinery but does not include, inter alia, computers or computer software.

(v) It is proposed to amend section 54 GB so as to provide that the expression 'new asset' includes computers or computer software in case of technology-driven start- ups so certified by the Inter-Ministerial Board of Certification notified by the Central Government. These amendments will take effect from 1st April 2017 and will, accordingly, apply in relation to the assessment year 2017-18, and subsequent assessment years.

(vi) The Budget has also indicated that it is envisaged to establish a Fund-of-Funds which intends to raise ₹ 2,500 crore annually for four years to finance start-ups the corpus is of ₹ 10,000 crore over four years. This will promote creation of start-up eco system in the country.

Start-up opportunities

ISRO looks to space start-ups

Opportunities for start-ups can be identified in a number of directions, where the use of innovation-driven technologies is of high priority. One area is opened by Indian Space Research Organisation (ISRO). The Biennial Space Conference and Expo was organised by ISRO in collaboration with Antrix Corporation, ISRO's commercial company, and other related oraganisations at Bengaluru during 1-3 September 2016. In the space sector, the role of manufacturers in satellite-based programmes is being strengthened by inviting a number of space start-ups or entrepreneurs to develop space technologies, applications and products - even building small space craft and rocket systems. As the new face of an otherwise government-driven sector, start-ups hope to get a platform for themselves in this field. (*The Hindu*, Vijayawada edition, August 24, 2016).

S. Rakesh, Chairman and Managing Director of Antrix Corporation outlined the scope for start-ups in the space field as follows: In future, space will have an increasingly large role to play in many areas in our lives. Space commerce is going to increase phenomenally, and India has all ingredients required to become a major space player. But ISRO cannot do it alone; it is basically an R & D organisation. Industry should be able to play a major part in future, on the lines of the US or European space sectors. Some of the common satellite based technologies are DTH television, tele-communication, earth imaging disaster management, and farm advisory.

ISRO, he said, is looking at improving the role of established players who are already supplying systems and components to it, as also new entrants or start-ups that can get into a few activities that ISRO does at present. Technologies are available with ISRO, and are ready to be transferred to industry. New entrants need to discuss with ISRO personnel. He also mentioned a few areas where collaboration can be fruitful. Solar panels used to generate power on satellites will be needed in large numbers as small satellites are booming. Makers of commercial solar panel will need to step up to space grade. For start-ups, sensors can be a low cost entry point. On the larger side, ISRO has larger launch vehicles and high throughput satellites in the offing which need industry support. Start-ups should be ideally prepared to invest in all related areas.

Public Procurement Policy (PPP) 2012

Availability of sub-contracting option under public procurement policy can be used by central public sector units (CPSUs) to encourage procurement from micro and small enterprises (MSEs), even if they continue to purchase from large suppliers. Making use of the opportunities available from CPSUs for sub-contracting will ensure greater thrust on capacity building of the MSE sector. This direction encourages innovation and self-sufficiency by participating in the programmes of the futuristic core sectors like Defence, Space, Railways, Mining, Automobiles, Renewable Energy and Nuclear Energy. In Defence, large scale efforts are being made to indigenise the manufacture of components. Creation of MSME vendor base for the Defence sector is being pursued by organising MSME-DEF-EXPO events and through B 2 B meetings. Organising vender development programmes (VDPs) and special VDPs for specific sectors or CPSUs for facilitating MSEs to become part of the supply chain is being done regularly in different parts of the country by the National Small Industries Corporation (NSIC) and the MSME-Development Institutes under the Development Commissioner (MSME). NSIC offers single point registration system (SPRS) for increasing the supplier base through online registration at www.nsicsprsonline.com. E-procurement initiative of public procurement cell of Department of Expenditure, Ministry of Finance, GoI has helped in greater transparency, and standardisation of the tendering process across the country. The vendors can access the opportunity through e-procurement process. It also helps procurement agencies in procuring items of their requirement at competitive prices via http://eprocure.gov.in/cppp. Offset policy of the Government in case of procurement of the establishments of Defence, Space, Railways, and other CPSUs should give priority to MSMEs to act as vendors.

GoI has notified Public Procurement Policy (PPP) for MSEs 2012 under MSMED Act 2006, which is effective from 1st April 2012. It is available on the website of Development Commissioner (MSME) www.dcmsme.gov.in. Every Central Ministry/Department/PSU shall set an annual goal for procurement from the MSE sector at the beginning of the year, with the objective of achieving an overall procurement goal of minimum of 20 per cent of total annual purchases of products or services produced or rendered by MSEs from the latter in a period of three years. At the end of 3 years, the overall procurement goal of minimum 20 per cent has become mandatory from 1st April 2015. Another provision in the policy is that 4 per cent procurement (20% of 20%) is to be made from MSEs owned by SC/ST entrepreneurs. Non-conforming departments will be required to provide reasons for the same to the Review Committee set up under the Policy.

Private sector expertise for incubators to guide/handhold start-ups

To ensure professional management of government sponsored/funded incubators to provide necessary facilities for start-ups, the Government will create a policy and framework for setting up of incubators across the country in public-private partnership mode. The facilities to be provided in an incubator through industry- academia tie-ups for nurturing innovations in academic institutions include physical infrastructure involving large capital investment for equipment, testing facilities and necessary buildings, provision of mentor support, access to networks, access to market, etc. Skills required for operating the incubator need to be developed by the private sector in collaboration with the host academic institution. As part of Atal Innovation Mission, funding of incubators will be planned by NITI Aayog. Government of India ministries/departments associated with the establishment of incubators include the departments of Science and Technology, Bio-technology, Electronics and Information Technology, Higher Education, Industrial Policy and Promotion, and MSME. The Ministry of MSME has promoted incubators at prestigious educational institutions as part of the National Manufacturing Competitiveness Programme in recent years.

The initial thinking was to establish incubators in collaboration with premier educational institutions in the country. These include IITs, IIMs, NITs, and other renowned specialised scientific and technological institutions. In earlier years, science and technology parks and a few incubators were set up under the sponsorship of departments of Science and Technology and Bio-technology, and development banks such as SIDBI. Experiences in these locations will be taken into account while promoting new incubators. There are a number of states and union territories not having such institutions. There is also a possibility and demand for locating more than one incubator in a state. The incubators can also be supported by industry apart from being supported by academic institutions. The DIPP is of the opinion that experienced industry-linked universities, engineering colleges and other specialised institutions can also be considered for locating the proposed incubators to spread the network to a number of states, and to a few prominent locations in as many states as possible. Faculty involvement of these institutions with appropriate expertise constitutes the base for selecting the thrust area for the incubator. Incubators need to co-opt experts in various areas of specialisation from nearby areas to cope with the demand from prospective entrepreneurs.

Compliance regime based on self-certification in respect of nine labour and environment laws will be adopted, and there will be no inspection during the first three years of the launch of the venture. Also, a liberalised patent regime is being brought in to help start-up businesses to register patents, for which the fee will be slashed by 80 per cent. The Start-up India Hub facilitates creation of a single point of contact for the entire start-up eco system, and enables knowledge exchange and access to funding. The Start-up India Hub will be a key stakeholder in this vibrant eco system. It will work in a hub and spoke model, and collaborate with the central and state governments, Indian and foreign venture capitalists, angel networks, banks, incubators, legal partners, consultants, universities, and R & D institutions.

Start-ups will be supported for bagging government procurement contracts by waiving the criteria of experience and turnover. Notification has already been issued for this purpose. The Corporate Affairs Department promised that they are working on a software in which registration of new ventures would be made possible within 24 hours. On 31st March, 2016, DIPP unveiled a start-up India portal, a start-up India hub, and a mobile app, besides setting up a panel to verify the eligibility of start-ups to avail of benefits. These will facilitate registration of start-ups within a day through mobile app, and apply for clearances online. Faster exit by failed ventures with a provision for winding them up within 90 days has been proposed under the Insolvency and Bankruptcy Code passed by the Parliament in May 2016 (details at Appendix-III) The Bankruptcy Code will improve the ease of doing business in the country. A simple and effective insolvency law is important for expediting the winding up of a company, selling its assets, and also for revival of sick companies. Easier entry and exit norms are important for start-ups, as there is a likelihood of a number of them failing in view of the uncertainties the companies face. Innovation for start-ups can also mean in the areas of frugal engineering, using less energy, less water, and keeping the air clean.

The incubation centres in India have not only grown in numbers and geographic spread, but also in terms of creating a dynamic support system to foster entrepreneurship, enhanced levels of innovation, and employment generation. Requisite skills for operating an incubator and enterprise development need to be developed in higher educational institutions, Innovation and Entrepreneurship Development Centres, and other centres dealing with technology and research and development. Prominent TBIs established in the last 15 years are: Technology Business Incubator in Delhi, SIDBI Innovation and Incubation Centre at IT-Kanpur, and Society for Innovation and Development at the Indian Institute of Science, Bengaluru, which is one of the oldest institutions in the country associated with entrepreneurship promotion. Most of the top business schools and technical schools offer entrepreneurship education in the form of short and long duration programmes. The IT-Madras Incubation Cell, called iCreate, consists of alumni dedicated to providing funding along with technical and business mentoring needed for a start-up to succeed. iCreate is an autonomous centre to facilitate a wide range of Next Generation entrepreneurs along with a vibrant eco system.

The Office of the Development Commissioner (MSME) has been implementing a scheme,"Support for Entrepreneurial and Managerial Development of SMEs through Incubators," which is also an initiative towards 'Make in India' efforts. The main objective of the scheme is to promote emerging technological and knowledge based innovative ventures that seek nurturing of ideas from professionals beyond the traditional activities of MSMEs. Such entrepreneurial ideas need to be tapped, fostered and developed in a supportive environment before they become attractive for venture capitalists. Hence the need arises for incubation centres to promote and support untapped creativity of individual innovators, and to assist them to become technology based entrepreneurs. The incubational support will be provided by host institutions, such as prominent educational and research institutions. Financial assistance provided by the government is between ₹ 4 and ₹ 8 lakh per idea/unit (on an average ₹ 6.25 lakh per idea/ unit) limited to ₹ 62.5 lakh for 10 ideas/units per host institution/ business incubator per year. The contribution of the incubator towards incubation of new innovative ideas shall be 15 per cent of the project cost for micro enterprises, and 25 per cent for small enterprises. While submitting ideas for financial support, it should be borne in mind that the idea should have been developed and likely to be completed into a marketable venture within a year.

National Innovation Foundation (NIF) under the Department of Science and Technology located in Ahmedabad, helps grass-root innovators and outstanding traditional knowledge holders get due recognition, respect and reward for their innovations. It also tries to ensure that such innovations diffuse widely through commercial and/or non-commercial channels, generating material or non-material incentives for the entrepreneurs involved in the value chain. Micro Venture Innovation Fund (MVIF) at NIF is in operation with the support of SIDBI to provide risk capital for entrepreneurs.

Building innovation centres at national institutions

To propel successful innovation through augmentation of incubation and R&D efforts, the Government plans

(a) To set up / scale up 31 innovation and entrepreneurship centres (to provide facilities for over 1,200 new start-ups) at national institutes

(b) To set up 13 start-up centres with annual funding of ₹ 50 lakh (shared by DST and MHRD - Ministry of Human Resource Development - on 50:50 basis) for encouraging student-driven start-ups from the host institute.

(c) To set up / scale up 18 technology business incubators at leading educational institutes.

Setting up of new research parks

Seven new research parks are modelled on the lines of the Research Park at IIT- Madras with an initial investment of ₹ 100 crore each. These will be in IITs located at Guwahati, Hyderabad, Kanpur, Kharagpur, Gandhinagar, and Delhi, and Indian Institute of Science in Bengaluru. These will create a collaborative environment between industry and academia through joint research projects and consulting assignments.

Promoting start-ups in the bio-technology sector

The Department of bio-technology endeavours to scale up a number of start-ups in the sector by nurturing 300 to 500 new start-ups each year to have around 2,000 start-ups by 2020. The programme is being implemented by the Department along with its public sector undertaking, Bio-technology Research Assistance Council (BIRAC). Five new bio-clusters, 50 new bio-incubators, 150 technology transfer offices, and 20 bio-connect offices will be set up in research institutes and universities across the country.

Launching of innovation focussed programmes for students

To foster a culture of innovation in the field of science and technology amongst students, a number of initiatives will be taken: (a) Innovation care to target school kids, (b) National initiative for developing and harnessing innovations (NIDHI) to be implemented through Innovation and Entrepreneurship Development Centres, (c) Uchhatar Avishkar Yojana for fostering very high quality research among IIT students.

Annual incubator grand challenge

This initiative aims at supporting creation of successful world class incubators in the country, and make them role models for other incubators.

DST initiatives in S&T led entrepreneurship and innovation promotion

The NSTEDB (National Science and Technology Entrepreneurship Development Board) of DST has taken several measures to foster and nurture innovation and entrepreneurship by scouting for and supporting innovative ideas, implementing various institutional programmes, and organising capacity building programmes across the country. In addition, the Department has also played an active role in formulating and enforcing a few policy interventions for strengthening technology business incubators and their start-ups. DST and Ministry of Human Resource Development (MHRD), GoI have launched a joint initiative of promoting start-up eco system in national institutes of repute. DST has been promoting establishment of Technology Business Incubators, and MHRD has been establishing research parks in different parts of the country in association with reputed educational institutions. Under this joint initiative, it is proposed to establish a 'Start-up Centre', a 'Technology Business Incubator'or a 'Research Park'depending on the preparedness of the institution in commercialisation of technologies, supporting industrial research, and nurturing and mentoring start-ups. It is proposed that the research parks shall be funded by MHRD, TBIs by DST, and Start-up Centres shall be jointly funded by DST & MHRD (on 50:50 basis). IIT-Hyderabad and IIT-Gandhinagar have been recommended for establishing research parks, 11 IITs/NITs have been recommended for establishing

TBIs, and 10 IITs/IIITs have been recommended for initiating Start- up Centres. Over years, DST has established 90 TBIs and Science and Technology Parks (STEPs), and several of them have matured, and developed competence to become state-of-the art incubators. Incubators have become a key mechanism for spurring entrepreneurial culture in institutions, introduction of innovative technologies in Society, and contribution to economic growth and employment generation. (Source: *DST Annual Report* 2015-16, New Delhi)

Stand-up India scheme

Under Stand-up India scheme, greater emphasis will be on promoting entrepreneurship among women and SC/STs. The scheme's motive is to make youth job creators from being job seekers. Implementation of the scheme will lead to greater degree of inclusive growth. It is targeted that each bank branch in the country, particularly in rural and semi-urban areas, provide loan for at least two such projects in a year, one for each category of entrepreneurs. A provision of ₹ 500 crore has been made for it in the Union Budget 2016-17. The scheme will benefit at least 2.5 lakh entrepreneurs during 2016-17. The entrepreneurs can avail of the facilities offered under various schemes being implemented for skill development and entrepreneurship. While celebrating the 125th birth anniversary of Dr. B.R. Ambedkar, the Government of India has declared 2016-17 as the year of empowerment of SC/ST entrepreneurs'. A National Scheduled Caste and Scheduled Tribe Hub has been created in the Office of the Development Commissioner (MSME) in partnership with industry associations. This Hub will provide professional support to SC/ST entrepreneurs in a number of directions to adopt global best practices.

Under MUDRA Yojana, loans up to ₹ 10 lakh will be granted to SC/ST and woman entrepreneurs to set up their businesses on hassle free terms. The overall intent of the scheme for under-served sections of the population is for facilitating bank loans repayable up to seven years, and between ₹ 10 lakh and ₹ 100 lakh for green-field enterprises in the non-farm sector by such SC/ST and woman borrowers. MUDRA Bank (Micro Units Development and Refinance Agency Bank), started in April 2015, offers loans under three categories - Shishu for loans up to 50,000 for start-ups; Kishor with above ₹ 50,000 and upto 5 lakh for mid-stage needs; and Tarun with above ₹ 5 lakh and upto 10 lakh for growth seekers.

The Bank gives priority to sanctioning loans in the shishu category, as it primarily deals with new micro enterprises. The other schemes are oriented towards expansion of projects and, in a limited way, for bigger new projects. The Bank is visualised as a boon to small business enthusiasts, particularly in rural and interior parts of the country. MUDRA card and credit enhancement are on the anvil for inclusion later. The Bank has been created with a corpus of ₹ 20,000 crore, and a credit guarantee fund of ₹ 3,000 crore, and functions as a subsidiary of SIDBI.

In order to foster smooth implementation of Stand-up India scheme, SIDBI developed a web portal, www.standupmitra.in which is designed to obtain application forms, provide information, enable registrations, provide links for handholding, tracking, and monitoring. This will enable the entire banking system to fulfil the intended objective of providing bank loans between ₹ 10 lakh and ₹ 1 crore to at least one SC or ST borrower and at least one woman borrower per bank branch in a year for setting up a green-field enterprise. This portal acts as a loan market place for application filing and tracking as well as providing the facility for choice of branches/banks for credit assistance. (Source: *SIDBI Annual Report* 2015-16, Lucknow)

Progress of incubators in Andhra Pradesh

The vision of the new Innovation and Start-up Policy of Government of Andhra Pradesh for 2014-20 reads as follows:

> "To create 'a world class technology start-up eco-system' by fostering entrepreneurship and a culture of innovation' which contributes to increased knowledge, wealth and employment in our society".

In line with the decision at the national level declaring 2010-20 as the decade of innovation, Andhra Pradesh government has set up an Innovation and Capacity Building Mission for implementing the policy of Re-imagining Andhra Pradesh - Role of E-governance, Electronics and IT (available on www.ap.gov.in). The government aims to make at least one person e-literate in each household. Through this policy, the state intends to create an eco system that produces entrepreneurial culture in every family, developing the following facilities to produce the desired results by June 2019.

- 100 incubators/accelerators to be established
- 5,000 companies/start-ups to be incubated
- Ten lakh sq. feet of incubation space to be developed
- Venture capital of ₹ 1,000 crore to be mobilised for innovation

- Foster innovation culture
- Create at least one home grown billion dollar technology start-up.

The niche themes being considered as focus areas are as follows:

- Internet of Things (IoT)
- 'IT for X'in the areas of pharma, oil and gas, and urban management
- Social media, mobility, analytics and cloud computing (SMAC)
- Cables semi-conductors
- Animation and gaming
- Entertainment
- Visual effects
- Health and fitness
- Automotive

The new policy of innovation would base itself on five pillars, viz., shared infrastructure, accelerators / incubators, human capital, funding and, above all, a system of governance (state support). The government shall establish at least one world class accelerator/incubator by inviting global accelerators/incubators to introduce their programmes in the state. It will also support the establishment of small accelerators/incubators in multiple locations in the state. Through industry- academia collaboration, these institutions will develop trained manpower in emerging technologies to promote innovators and techno-preneurs among the youth.

The government shall develop physical incubation infrastructure through public-private-partnerships. A new incubation infrastructure fund will be set up under the innovation mission as a revolving fund that provides conditional grant for the special purpose vehicle (SPV), promoted by the host institute of the technology business incubator, and approved by NSTEDB, Department of Science and Technology, Government of India. An Innovation and Transformation Academy will be set up for fostering innovation in the state. Through leadership and entrepreneurship training programmes, entrepreneurship culture will be institutionalised in different parts of the state. An initial innovation fund of ₹ 100 crore will be created for entrepreneurs and businesses. The fund will be in the nature of fund of funds. It does not invest directly in start-up companies. It shall participate in the capital of Securities and Exchange Board of India (SEBI) approved venture capital (VC) funds, with up to 15 per cent, as a limited partner. The VC fund in turn is free to invest in start-ups located in different parts of the state, based on their appraisal criteria. The fund will also support a number of activities in this programme including establishment of pilot incubators.

The other important contribution of the state government is to offer non-fiscal and fiscal incentives to start-up entities. A highly empowered single window clearance unit will be created and operationalised for granting approvals and clearances to primarily first time and young entrepreneurs. The Andhra Pradesh Innovation Council would be formed. Apart from incentives normally available for micro, small and medium enterprises, special incentives will be made available for IT and other specialised categories of enterprises, taking into account their needs. Women and SC/ST entrepreneurs will be given additional incentives. IT units in rural areas will derive special advantages. For various product groups, based on the nature of activity, tailor-made facilities and incentives will be offered.

The progress of implementing the IT policy for start-up companies in the IT and IT enabled services and allied sectors in Andhra Pradesh is briefly reviewed here. Locations identified for incubator towers are Visakhapatnam, Kakinada and Tirupati. Incubator towers are already commissioned. Visakhapatnam has two towers, and Kakinada and Tirupati one each. In Visakhapatnam, incubation tower at Rushikonda, built by Andhra Pradesh Industrial Infrastructure Corporation (APIIC), started functioning from December 2014 under the guidance of Kochi (Kerala) based pilot incubator Mob Mee start-up village which pioneered the start-up concept. In Kakinada where the incubation tower is operating under the guidance of the Bhubaneswar based private pilot incubator KIIT-TBI, 25 start-up companies have started functioning. Tirupati incubation tower with 15,000 sq.ft is functioning under the guidance of the pilot incubator Venus Geo.

A start-up unit comprising fresh and final year engineering graduates will take on an average about two years to work on their product and idea before it can attract the attention of venture capitalists and angel investors. While three companies are ready for tie-ups with start-up units in Visakhapatnam incubation tower, AP government which invested on incubation towers has placed a condition that the mature start-ups should base their companies in the state, whoever might be their venture capitalist.

The mandate of the empanelled incubators is to promote the culture of innovation among the start-up units while the state is looking at creating a world class eco-system, and lay a strong foundation to make a mark in IT product development. Recently, Intel and C-Dac organised training programmes for the start-ups in Visakhapatnam working on ideas and products related to their domain expertise. The government has also been extending some financial assistance to the pilot incubator on behalf of each start-up unit for organising training praogrammes, and promoting products and ideas, once they reach a certain stage of development, to attract venture capitalists and angel investors. The Rushikonda facility is known as Technology, Research and Innovation Park. In Visakhapatnam, another five- floor tower, named as Millennium Tower of three lakh sq. ft. space will come up on a four-acre land adjacent to the Rushikonda Incubation Tower. The first two floors will be for start-up units, and the other three floors will be allotted to companies.

Conclusion

The article has presented the directions to be pursued in respect of two innovative programmes in entrepreneurship development: Start-up India and Stand-up India, as complementary to the Make in India campaign. The first refers to innovative entrepreneurship based on research and development, and experiments carried out in technology business incubators, with the support of a host institution. The second refers to inclusiveness of promoting entrepreneurship among women, and SC/ST candidates in particular, in rural and semi-urban areas, and remote and less developed regions. In the context of start-up entities as per the definition specifically spelt out for availing fiscal, financial, and other incentives and benefits, entrepreneurs should develop the products and processes, experiment on a smaller or laboratory scale, and be prepared to face high risk, before launching a product on commercial scale. In view of the high risk involved, angel investors and venture capitalists support such ventures, and government extends support in various ways. Conventional loans from development and commercial banks can be utilised after the enterprise is reasonably well established. Apart from supporting research and development, early entry and early exit, and creation of liberal eco system, establishment of fund-of-funds for providing equity, quasi-equity and development loans on relatively soft terms are important roles of the government. The fund-of- funds created for different product groups is utilised for extending loans to venture capital companies to enable them to meet the equity and developmental loan requirements of start-up entities. Opportunities available from sectors such as Space, Defence, Railways, Renewable energy, and Nuclear energy need to be utilised by the youth to promote risky start-up entities. Public procurement policy is another direction for registering themselves as vendors to Central Public Sector Units for availing the benefits. Strategies outlined are essentially through technology business incubators and research parks promoted in collaboration with leading educational and scientific research institutions. Joint efforts of industry and academia, with the appropriate eco system and support created by the government can pave the way for more enlightened entrepreneurship to ensure the success of start-ups.

Appendix - I: Global Hardware Start-Up Accelerator Eyeing India

*(**Source:*** The Hindu, *Vijayawada edition, 20th July 2016)*

HAX, the world's largest hardware start-up accelerator, is scouting for investments in young firms in India, which have developed working prototypes in areas such as health care, consumer electronics, robotics, and bionics.

Benjamin Joffe, general partner at the Shenzhen (China) based HAX said that he has met founders of at least ten Indian hardware start-ups in Bengaluru to explore investment opportunities. These firms have developed various hardware products such as roti machine, car head-up display, baby monitoring system, and robotic cocktail machine.

"There is a lot of talent in India, but it is very difficult to go beyond the first (hardware) prototype," said Joffe in an interview. I think connecting Indian creation, engineering and science with Shenzhen (China) and the Silicon Valley (USA) is the way to go, he added. The Chinese accelerator would invest seed capital of US $ 100,000 in each firm in return for 9 per cent stake, and also invest in follow-on rounds. He said, selected teams would go through a four-month training programme at its offices in Shenzhen and the Silicon Valley. They would get access to mentorship, a shared office and lab space, and specialised staff to help with design and sourcing.

The accelerator is backed by US-based venture firm SOSV which has a corpus of US $250 million. "The challenge is to find start-ups that not only have good technology, that is hard to copy, but are also targeting a large market, and are different from what already exists", said Joffe. Founded in 2011, the founders of HAX are best known for co-founding Map Info Corporation, and for coining the term cloud computing. HAX has invested in over 150 start-ups.

When Joffe came to know that Bengaluru has the biggest community for Internet of Things (IoT) - a technology where devices communicate with each other intelligently, it caught his attention. Joffe stated that he discovered that Internet of Things Bengaluru (IOTBLR) has now become the largest IoT- focused meet-up group in the world, followed by similar communities in London, San Francisco, Paris, and New York.

Appendix - II: SBI Incube - First start-up focused bank branch

State Bank of India (SBI) launched on 14 January 2016 and inaugurated the country's first start-up focused bank branch called SBI InCube in Bengaluru (Karnataka). The specialised branch aims at understanding and addressing the banking needs of start-up businesses. The Bank also launched the wealth management service, SBI Exclusive, which is targeted at the fast growing affluent segment of the economy. InCube in Bengaluru will be headed by an assistant general manager, and a team of three other officers. It will soon open branches in Pune and New Delhi.

The InCube branch, in its current form, will not fund start-ups, i.e., it will not provide loans at present. However, when the start-ups become mature and continue to progress, this branch will give them loan. The branch will work towards fulfilling the specific financial needs of the start-ups; it will provide advisory services to budding entrepreneurs under one roof. It will assist start-ups in cash management, regulations, taxation, mentoring, foreign exchange and remittances, and other financial services. The entrepreneurs will be helped to solicit support of angel investors and venture capitalists for obtaining funds under liberal terms.

Appendix - III: Insolvency and Bankruptcy Code passed by the Parliament

(Source: Yojana, *60 (6), June 2016: 67.)*

The historic Insolvency and Bankruptcy Code, 2016 was passed by the Parliament on 11th May 2016. The legislation aims to consolidate the laws relating to insolvency of companies and limited liability entities (including limited liability partnerships and individuals, presently contained in a number of legislations, into a single legislation. Such consolidation will provide for greater clarity in law, and facilitate the application of consistent and coherent provisions to different stakeholders affected by business failure or inability to pay debt.

A few of the salient features of the law are listed here.

(i) Clear, coherent and speedy process for early identification of financial distress and resolution of companies and limited liability entities if the underlying business is found to be viable.

(ii) Two distinct processes for resolution of individuals, namely, 'fresh start' and 'Insolvency resolution'.

(iii) Debt Recovery Tribunal and National Company Law Tribunal to act as Adjudicating Authority, and deal with the cases related to insolvency, liquidation, and bankruptcy process in respect of individuals and unlimited partnership firms, and in respect of companies and limited liability entities, respectively.

(iv) Establishment of an Insolvency and Bankruptcy Board of India to exercise regulatory over-sight over insolvency professionals, insolvency professional agencies, and information utilities.

(v) Insolvency professionals would handle the commercial aspects of insolvency resolution process. Insolvency professional agencies will develop professional standards, code of ethics, and be first level regulator for insolvency professionals members leading to development of a competitive industry for such professionals.

(vi) Information utilities would collect, collate, authenticate, and disseminate financial information to be used in insolvency liquidation and bankruptcy proceedings.

(vii) Enabling provisions to deal with cross border insolvency.

A key innovation of the present Code is four pillars of institutional infrastructure. These are: (a) A class of regulated persons, the insolvency professionals: They would be regulated by insolvency professional agencies; (b) Information utilities: these would store facts about lenders and terms of lending in electronic databases; (c) Adjudication: NCLT and DRTs, along with their appellate bodies, viz., NCLAT and DRATs will be adequately strengthened; (d) Regulator, the Insolvency and Bankruptcy Board of India. The Code is, thus, a comprehensive and systematic reform, which will give a quantum leap to the functioning of the credit market. It lays the foundations for the development of the corporate bond market, which would finance infrastructure projects of the future. The passing of this code and implementation of the same will give a big boost to ease of doing business in India.

10

Rural Fisherwoman Entrepreneurs and Their Problems with Special Reference to North Andaman

– *B.S.V. Meera Setty*

In the words of Pandit Jawaharlal Nehru, "When women move forward, the family moves, the villages move and the whole country moves".

Abstract

The entrepreneur is an economic man or woman who may try to maximise their profits by innovation. Innovation involves problem solving, introduction of new things or making changes in the pattern of goods and services or taking initiative to develop their business and activities. There are around seven lakh villages in India, in which more than 70 per cent of our population lives, and half of them are women. Rural women represent a sizeable percentage of labour force in our country. The rural women play a vital role in developing their family in all aspects - like development of children, support to her husband, development of her home, better society and better livelihood.

Entrepreneurship is the core of economic development and entrepreneur is its key factor. In the present time women are an emerging economic force. Social and economic development of women is necessary for the development of any country. Every woman wants to start her own business but cannot succeed in the Indian environment due to male domination in the family and in society. Due to changing environment, men are now easily accepting women in entrepreneurial opportunity. The expanding service sector, production sector, Central and state government policies are promoting woman entrepreneurship.

Keywords: *Rural fisherwoman entrepreneurs, concept of woman entrepreneur, economic status*

The aim of this study is to discuss the role of rural fisherwoman entrepreneurs in the rural Andaman region of Mayabunder tehsil. The study may focus on the pattern of fisherwomen's families, their income, economic status, marketing of fish produce and livelihood of their families, and assistance from various agencies. This paper is mostly based on primary data and some observations. For the identification of these issues the author has reviewed different research articles.

Methodology

The present study was conducted at Mayabunder fishermen colony, Mayabunder tehsil, North and Middle Andaman district. The whole study is based on primary data. A questionnaire has been prepared about the personal profile of fisherwomen, economic status, their culture and traditions, and their role, and the problems being faced by the target group. A total of 65 questionnaires were prepared and distributed to the fisherwomen for collecting primary data and 55 respondents had shown interest and given answers to the questionnaire and submitted. Among the 55 questionnaires collected from the respondents, five respondents' questionnaires were incomplete and were not taken for study. Only 50 respondents data were taken for study. The sample was analysed by using simple average and ratio method.

Review of literature

Mehta A. and Mehta M.C., in their article, "Rural Women Entrepreneurship in India- Opportunities and Challenges" (2011), revealed that rural women were not so aware and literate to handle all the legal and other formalities to set up enterprise or entrepreneurship. In their study they said that the literacy rate of women in India was low as compared to male population. Women entrepreneurs were not so developed due to less ability to bear risk and risk taking, lack of infrastructure, lack of finance and knowledge about various schemes. In their study they suggested that better educational facilities, training, counselling, micro credit facilities, marketing assistance and guidance cell to be set up for the purpose of effective development of woman entrepreneurs.

Sharma Y. (2013) in her study on "Women Entrepreneur in India", focused on problems faced by woman entrepreneurs: Indian women are very emotional and attached to their family members, male dominated society, lack of education, social barriers, shortage of raw materials, lack of finance, tough competition with male dominated entrepreneurship, etc.

In her study she has given an account of steps taken by the Goverment of India in the five year plans. She concluded that India is a male dominated society and women socially and economically depended on the male members. So Government and other agencies and family members may encourage and support woman entrepreneurs to become a main part of national economy and contribute to the economic progress of India.

Objectives of the study

(a) To find out the economic status of families of fisherwomen of Mayabunder Tehsil

(b) To analyse the influencing factors to do business (selling of fish)

(c) To study the economic and other support given by various agencies

(d) To study the problems facing by fisherwomen entrepreneur

Concept of woman entrepreneurs

Women entrepreneurs may be defined as a woman or a group of women who initiate, organise and operate a business enterprise. The Government of India has defined women entrepreneurs as ‾an enterprise owned and controlled by women having a minimum financial interest of 51 per cent of the capital and giving at least 51 per cent of the employment generated in the enterprise to women. Women entrepreneurs engaged in business due to push and pull factors which encourage women to have an independent occupation and stand on their own feet.

Status of women in historical perspective

"Freedom depends more on economic conditions than on political. If a woman is not economically free and self-earning, she will have to depend on her husband or someone eels and dependents are never free", the then first Prime Minister of India Pt. Jawaharlal Nehru said, highlighting the importance of economic independence of women.

The history says that women in the Vedic age had played an important part in religious and social functions. The position of wife was an honoured one as no religious ceremony could be performed by the husband alone.

Modern rural woman

But the modern rural women are not like women of the Vedic age. They are coming out from their houses and working as past of work-force in various organisations and agencies same as men, giving a supporting hand to their families. They are mostly working in government departments, private organisations, manufacturing industries, schools, hotels, and government schemes like MGNREGA and other part- time jobs. A few women set up their own businesses like tea and snacks shops, retail shops, fancy stores, bakery shops, beauty parlours, vegetable selling, fish vending, etc.

History of fisherwoman entrepreneurs of Mayabunder tehsil

Mayabunder tehsil is one of the rural areas of the North and Middle Andaman district, Andaman and Nicobar Islands, but is connected with Port Blair by road, sea and airway (helicopter) and also connected to the mainland (Kolkata) by waterway. Mayabunder is the district headquarter of North and Middle Andaman district.

Most of the fishermen and women of Mayabunder tehsil have migrated from the rural backward district of Srikakulam of Andhra Pradesh and the east-south part of Odisha. Srikaklulam district is industrially backward and is one of the most un- developed regions of the state of Andhra Pradesh. The paddy land and other land is too dry and sandy which is difficult to farm. Also, they may not get sufficient water for farming and the fishermen community find difficulties in venturing into the sea to catch fish in the coastal area of Srikakulam district, due to heavy waves in sea and lack of professional equipments like boats and nets. In the early 1960s and 1970s, most of them had migrated and travelled from Srikakulam to Andaman in search of employment. These people have settled in many parts of the Andaman and Nicobar Islands. A few have settled in the South Andaman district at - Dairyfarm Port Blair, Haddo, Wandoor, Hut bay, etc. A few others are at the North and Middle Andaman district - Diglipur, Areial bay, Kalighat (two or three families), Mayabunder, Rangat bay, Betapur (Haroro), Ireata, Long Island, and Baratang Island. Very few families have settled at Hut bay and the southern most island of Chambell bay (Great Andaman).

Many of them have migrated in the late 1960s and 1970s, and slowly settled in different parts of the Island. In those days of the post-Independence period the fishermen and women worked as mazdoor or labour in various departments and organisations until the 1990s.

The fishermen community may have started catching fish for their own use - for their family consumption - in the early 1970s. But after the 1970s they started selling the fish in the markets, villages and other places.

This practice has prompted them to do business and earn some money to look after their family members.

The fisherwomen of the present study had started their business activities in late 1990. Very few fisherwomen go with their husbands and venture into the sea for catching fish, but most of them are fish vendors. They usually purchase fish in lump sum from fishermen and they sell the same in different localities or villages of Mayabunder tehsil. They can be found in the Mayabunder bazaar area and the fish market of Mayabunder. Early morning at 4.00 am they carry fish in utensils, to Harinagar , Nimbudera, Karmatang, Rampur, Burmdera, Lucknow and other parts of Mayabunder tehsil in a bus or van or small truck used for selling the fish. The fisherwomen are very shy, traditional and honest in their business activities. Their families follow their own traditions and cultural activities; they unite in all functions and respect each other.

Role of fisherwoman entrepreneurs

Fisherwoman entrepreneurs are supporting their families and family members in all aspects. They sell the fish which has been caught by their husbands and family members and friends in different places of Mayabunder tehsil. They earn income for their family and help the husband. They play the important role of selling and marketing the fish and fish products. Fisherwomen save money by opening savings bank account in the SBI and in the State Co-operative Bank Limited, Mayabunder. They look after, and help and support their children in education and other areas. The fisherwoman entrepreneurs play an important role in the overall development of their family members and their community.

Scope of the study

The present study may be useful in taking various measures and policy decisions regarding development and economic status of fishermen and fisherwomen in Andaman and Nicobar Islands.

Table - 10.1: Age group and marital status of fisherwomen

Sl. No.	*Marital status*	*Age in years*				*Total*
		18 to 25yrs	*25 to 30yrs*	*30 to 35yrs*	*35 and above*	
1	Married	0	05 (10%)	12 (24%)	33 (66%)	50
2	Unmarried	0	0	0	0	0
Total		**0**	**05**	**12**	**33**	

Table-10.1 shows the age group and marital status of fisherwomen. It shows that all (100 %) respondents were married and maximum (66%) respondents belonged to above 35 years group. It gives clear picture that the fisherwomen who engage in selling fish in various places are married. It means that no unmarried fisherwomen were engaged in this activity.

Table - 10.2: Marital status and educational qualifications of fisherwomen

Sl No	*Marital status*	*Educational qualification*				*Total*
		Illiterate	*Primary*	*Secondary*	*Sr. Sec. Education*	
1	Married	38 (76 %)	08 (16%)	04 (8%)	0	50
2	Unmarried	0	0	0	0	0
Total		**38**	**08**	**04**	**0**	**50**

Source : Primary data.

Table-10.2 shows that marital status and educational qualification of the respondents. All respondents were married. In respect of their qualification, 38 (76%) were illiterate and other respondents had studied up to primary and secondary levels. Only 8 respondents (16%) had primary education and the remaining 4 (8%) respondents had studied up to secondary education.

Table - 10.3: Push factors for choosing business

Sl No	*Particulars / factors*	*No. of respondents*	*(%)*
1.	Self (Family financial problem)	20	40
2.	Parents	7	14
3.	Relatives	7	14
4.	Family Members	10	20
5.	Friends	4	8
6.	Awareness programmes	0	0
7.	Family background	02	4
8.	Others (specify)	0	0

Source : Primary data.

Table-10.3 shows the push factors for engaging in selling of fish by the respondents. The major factor that pushed the respondents into this activity was the family financial problem. The above table indicates that almost 20 respondents (40%) were engaged in this activity due to their family condition, and financial problems and other factors. Family members (20%) too had pushed the respondents to engage in this activity. The remaining factors like parents, relatives, family background, etc were also having push impact on the respondents to engage in selling of fish and fish products in the market.

Table - 10.4: Capital invested in fish business by respondents' family members

Sl. No.	*Capital invested*	*Invested in business activities*			
		Mechanised boat	*Non-mechanised boat*	*Ice box*	*Fishing net*
1.	Less than ₹ 50,000	0	20 (40 %)	18 (36%)	45(90%)
2.	₹ 50,000 to 1 Lakh	0	05 (10 %)	0	0
3.	I Lakh to 1.5 Lakh	09 (18 %)	0	0	0
4.	1.5 Lakh to 2 Lakh	05 (10 %)	0	0	0
5.	2 lakh & Above	03 (6%)	0	0	0
Total		**17 (34%)**	**25 (50%)**	**18 (36%)**	**45 (90%)**

Source: Primary data.

Table-10.4 indicates the capital invested in business for purchasing mechanised dingy non-mechanised dingy, ice box and fishing net by the respondents. A total of 17 (34%) respondents' family members had mechanised boats from among 50, and it includes a total of 9 (18%) who invested ₹ 1 lakh to ₹ 1.5 lakh and 8 respondents who invested more than ₹ 1.5 lakh for procuring of mechanised boats.

A total of 25 (50%) respondents family members had non-mechanised boats. Among them 20 (40%) respondents had invested less than ₹ 50,000 and 5 (10%) had invested between ₹ 50,000 and 1 lakh.

Table - 10.5: Average sales of fish per day and profit earned

Sl. No.	*Average sales per day*	*Profit earned*			*Total*
		₹200	*₹200 to ₹500*	*₹500 & Above*	
1.	Below ₹ 500	15	06	0	21(42%)
2.	₹ 500 to 1000	09	07	02	18(36%)
3.	₹ 1000 to ₹ 1500	02	04	0	06(12%)
4.	₹ 1500 & Above	0	3	2	05(10%)
Total		**26(52%)**	**20(40%)**	**04(8%)**	**50**

Source: Primary data.

Only 18 (36%) respondents had ice box for storage of fish products and they had invested an amount of less than ₹ 50,000; 45 (90%) respondents had fishing net for catching fish in the sea and they had invested a maximum of ₹ 50,000 for procuring fishing net.

Table-10.5 shows the average sales of fish per day and profit earned by respondents. Almost 52 per cent of respondents had average sales below ₹ 500 and 36 per cent respondents, average selling of fish was ₹ 500 to ₹ 1,000 per day, and 10 per cent respondents' average selling of fish was ₹ 1,500 and above. Concerning the profit earned per day, 26 per cent of respondents had earned ₹ 200, and 40 per cent respondents had earned a profit of ₹ 200 to 500.

Table - 10.6: Arrangement of capital (finance)

Sl No	*Particulars*	*Arrangement of Capital*					*Total*
		From Bank	*Financer (Money lenders)*	*Friends*	*Family members*	*Fisheries Dept.*	
1.	Less than ₹ 50,000	0 (0%)	10 (20%)	4 (8%)	3 (6%)	6 (12%)	23 (46%)
2.	₹ 50,000 to 1 lakh	5 (10%)	5 (10%)	3 (6%)	2 (4%)	3 (6%)	18 (36%)
3.	₹ 1 lakh to 1.5 Lakh	1 (2%)	3 (6%)	2 (1%)	0 (0%)	2 (1%)	08 (16%)
4.	₹ 1.5 lakh to 2 lakh	1 (2 %)	0 (0%)	0 (0%)	0 (0%)	0 (0%)	01 (2 %)
5.	₹ 2 Lakh & Above	0 (0%)	0 (0%)	0 (0%)	0 (0%)	0 (0%)	0 (0%)
		7 (14%)	18 (36%)	9 (18%)	5 (10%)	11 (22%)	50 (100%)

Source : Primary data.

Table-10.6 shows the arrangement of capital/finance by the fisherwomen. Of the respondents 18 (36 %) had obtained finance from money-lenders, including 10 (20%) who had obtained loan up to ₹ 50,000, while 5 (10%) and 3 (6%) respondents had obtained loan up to ₹ 50,000 to ₹ 1 lakh and ₹ 1 lakh to ₹ 1.5 lakh respectively from money-lenders. Besides 9 (18%) respondents had obtained loan from their friends, including 4 (8%) who had obtained a loan of ₹ 50,000, while 6 (12%) respondents had obtained loan up to ₹ 50,000 to 1 lakh, and 1 (2%) respondent had obtained a loan of ₹ 1 lakh to 1.5 lakh, from their friends.

Only 7 (14%) respondents had obtained loan from banks and 11 (22%) respondents had obtained loan from their friends.

Table - 10.7: EDP training and awareness programme provided by agencies

Sl No	*Agencies*	*EDP training attended*		*EDP awareness programme*		*Skill development programme*	
		Yes	*No*	*Yes*	*No*	*Yes*	*No*
1.	District Industries Center	5 (10%)	45 (90%)	5 (10 %)	45 (90%)	0 (0%)	50 (100%)
2.	KVIB	0 (0%)	50 (100%)	0	50 (100%)	0 (0%)	50 (100%)
3.	Bank	10 (20%)	45 (80%)	10 (20%)	45 (80 %)	0 (0%)	50 (100%)
4.	Fisheries Dept.	15 (30%)	35 (70%)	15 (30%)	35 (70%)	15 (30%)	35 (70%)
5.	Gram Panchayat	12 (24%)	38 (76 %)	12 (24%)	38 (76 %)	0 (0%)	50 (100%)

Source : Primary data.

Table-10.7 shows the entrepreneurial development programme and awareness programme conducted by various agencies. Respondents viewed that fisheries department (30%), gram panchayat (24%) and banks (20%) had conducted more number of EDP training and awareness programmes. In respect of skill development programmes, the respondents stated that only one agency, i.e., fisheries department (15%) had conducted it and the remaining agencies had not conducted any such programmes.

Table - 10.8: Subsidy for loan borrowed

Sl No	*Agencies*	*Subsidy for loan borrowed*		*Total*
		Yes	*No*	
1.	From bank	3 (6%)	4 (8%)	7 (14%)
2.	Friends	0 (0%)	9 (18 %)	9 (18%)
3.	Family members	0 (0%)	5 (10%)	5 (10%)
4.	Fisheries Dept.	7 (14%)	3 (6%)	11 (22%)
5.	Financer (money-lenders)	0 (0%)	18 (36%)	18 (36%)
	Total	**10 (20%)**	**40 (80%)**	**50 (100%)**

Source : Primary data.

Table-10.9 shows that the respondents received subsidy for loan borrowed from different agencies. Banks have provided loan subsidy to 3 (6%) respondents from among total seven, while the fisheries department had provided loan subsidy to 7 (14%) respondents from among total 11 respondents.

Table - 10.9: Respondents having own house or staying at rented house

Sl No	Particulars	*Type of house*			Total
		Pacca House	*Semi pacca house*	*Thatching and timber ropinghouses*	
1,	Own house	04 (8%)	08 (16%)	07 (14%)	19 (38 %)
2,	Rented house	03 (6%)	20 (40%)	08 (16%)	31(62 %)
Total		**07 (14%)**	**28(56 %)**	**15 (30 %)**	**50 (100%)**

Source : Primary data.

Table-10.9 shows whether the respondents had their own house or lived in a rented house. The data collected shows that 38 per cent of the respondents stayed in own houses which included 8 per cent pacca houses; 16 per cent semi-pacca houses and 14 per cent respondents were staying in thatching and timber roping houses. Most of the respondents, i.e., 62 per cent were staying in rented houses which included 6 per cent pacca houses, 40 per cent semi-pacca houses, and 16 per cent were staying in thatching and timber roping houses.

Table - 10.10: Knowledge about government schemes

Sl No	*Particulars*	*Yes*	*No*	*Total*
1.	PMEGP (Prime Minister employment Guarantee Programme)	05 (10 %)	45 (90%)	50 (100%)
2.	IAY (Indira Awas Yojana)	8 (16 %)	42 (34 %)	50 (100%)
3.	MGNREGA(Mahatama Gandhi National Rural Employment Guarantee ACT)	30 (60 %)	20 (40%)	50 (100%)
4.	NHRM (National Rural Health Mission)	06 (12 %)	44 (88%)	50 (100%)
5.	DRDA Schemes (District Rural Development Authority)	02 (4%)	48 (96 %)	50 (100%)

Source : Primary data.

Table-10.10 shows the information and knowledge of the respondents about various schemes of Central government: 60 per cent of the respondents knew about MGNREGA (Mahatama Gandhi National Rural Employment Guarantee ACT). Only 10 per cent of the respondents knew about the Prime Minister‘s Employment Guarantee Programme, 12 per cent of the respondents knew about National Rural Health Mission and 16 per cent of the respondents knew about Indira Awas Yojana.

Table - 10.11: Cold storage facilities

Sl. No.	*Particulars*	*Yes*	*No*	*Total*
1.	Ice box	28 (56 %)	22 (44%)	50 (100%)
2.	Cold storage room	0 (0%)	50 (100%)	50 (100%)
3.	Refrigerator	6 (12%)	44(88%)	50 (100%)

Source : Primary data.

Table-10.11 shows the cold storage facilities: 28 (56 %) respondents were having ice box facilities for storing fish and fish products, and 6 (12 %) respondents had refrigerator facilities. None of the respondents were having cold storage room facilities for storage of fish in large quantities.

Problems faced by fisherwoman entrepreneurs

(a) Illiterate

The study found that most of the respondents were illiterate. Nearly 76 per cent of the respondents were illiterate, and 16 per cent respondents had primary education, while 8 per cent had secondary education. It is one of the biggest problems among the fisherwoman entrepreneurs. They lack knowledge about various schemes and facilitates provided by various agencies and departments.

(b) Not aware about various schemes

The Central government, Andaman and Nicobar administration, fisheries department and district administration may provide various benefits through various schemes, but many of the respondents are not aware due to lack of information and illiteracy. About 70 per cent to 90 per cent of the respondents were not aware of the various schemes introduced by the Central government.

(c) Transportation problem

Nearly 80 per cent of the respondents stated that they had transportation problems. They are selling fish at different places and locations but they find it difficult to get bus, van, truck or cargo jeep facilities at the right time. Many times their fish deteriorate due to lack of transportation.

(d) Marketing problems

More than 100 women were selling fish at Mayabunder area and the remaining were selling fish at different places in and around Mayabunder tehsil. They were finding it difficult to go to different places every morning by bus or other mode of transport.

(e) Financial problems

Fisherwomen and their family members are weak in finance and they find it difficult to arrange finance for various purposes like purchasing mechanised boats for their family members, purchasing latest fishing net, purchasing cold storage facilities, installing GPS in their boats and for constructing a house. Most of the fishermen were dwelling in ruined houses.

(f) Cold storage and ice box facilities

Only 28 per cent of the respondents had ice box facility and 12 per cent had refrigerator facility. None of the respondents had cold storage room facilities for storage of fish in large quantities.

Suggestions

After the analysis of data, the following suggestions are made.

(a) A & N Administration, Fisheries department and other agencies should provide financial support to fisherwoman entrepreneurs and their family members for construction of houses, purchasing mechanised boats with GPS, and for purchasing modernised nets for catching fish.

(b) Mostly fishermen venture into sea for catching fish and it is full of risk. So, the administration and other departments may provide insurance for securing their life and family members. Insurance should be provided for their life, mechanised boats and non-mechanised boats, etc.

(c) Most of the respondents stated that they had transportation problems for carrying their fish and fish products to other locations and parts of Mayabunder tehsil. So, the administration and other departments may take steps to provide transportation facilities, or the fisheries department can also provide this logistic support by charging minimum tariff.

(d) Entrepreneurial development training should be provided to them for better marketing and knowledge about various services.

(e) Cold storage and ice box facilities should be provided at subsidised rates, which will help them to store the fish and its products.

(f) Housing facilities are to be provided to the fishermen community and subsidised housing loans should be provided to them to construct healthy houses.

(g) Most of the respondents have viewed that skill development and entrepreneurial development programmes were arranged and conducted rarely. These types of programmes are to be conducted frequently at grass-root level to the vulnerable groups, with the support of local authority.

(h) Many respondents stated that they had no knowledge about PMRY (Prime Minister's Rojgar Yojana), IAY (Indira Awas Yojana), DRDA scheme, NRHM scheme, etc. These schemes were among the flagship programme of the Central government. Therefore education and communication need to be provided to such groups.

(i) The study reveals that fisherwoman entrepreneurs had no idea or knowledge about the loan subsidy provided to them and their family members. Hence the district administration and local authority should take responsibility to make them aware of such schemes available to them.

11

Promoting Agri Business Start-ups Through Integrated Entrepreneurship Development Approach in Maharashtra: "Mantra" For Start-ups Every Year in Each Indian State

– *V. Padmanand*
Kunal Sood
M. Chandrashekar Reddy

Abstract

The entrepreneurship development approach in the agri business sector summarised in this paper presents an "ideal" approach towards selection of potential start-up candidates, their training, capacity building and guidance over preparation of a bankable business plan as well as on subsequent monitoring1. Other than tracing the approach and methodology of the intervention, this paper also presents case studies on successful start-ups facilitated using a related intervention frame-work in Maharashtra reflecting the rationale for start-up, entrepreneur profile, basic project parameters and demand conditions vis-a-vis the project. The cases considered present a mix in terms of entrepreneurs who have received a preliminary "Letter of Intent" (LoI) from financial institutions (virtually an in-principle sanction of loan facility), to those who also have recently been sanctioned loans as well as those who have commenced operations sustainably. This mix provides a flavour of diverse circumstances in these important stages of an enterprise start-up. The cases cover entrepreneurship in the agri business sector. Apparently, the agro and food processing industry has experienced consistent growth in demand over the last five years till 2016, as economies across the globe continued to consume processed fruits, vegetable and other food products in ever growing degree with ever increasing consumer spend. Notably, demand for processed food products has grown faster in the developing economies as industrial and economic growth has translated into greater levels of urbanisation, higher per capita incomes and expansion in the size of the middle-class. As the global "middle-class" segment has grown, it demands larger quantities of higher quality and more-diverse processed food. Despite the potential, the agro and food processing or agri business sector confronts a scenario of inadequate investment in post-harvest facilities, primary as well as secondary processing leading to losses ranging from 5 to30 per cent in different sub-sectors of the sector which is virtually a national loss. There is apparently a need for dedicated entrepreneurship development and start-up focused interventions to link entrepreneurs with sector potential for value- addition as well as employment generation. Notably, interventions along these lines are presently being undertaken successfully under the World Bank assisted Maharashtra Agricultural Competitiveness Project (MACP) by the Agri Business Promotion Facility (ABPF) operated by the Grant Thornton India LLP. About 660 start-ups are being catalysed and incubated to provide employment to at least 6,000 persons directly and indirectly. The start-ups are largely agro processing enterprises typically with investment in terms of project cost ranging from ₹15 lakh to ₹40 lakh. A few have also entailed investment of over ₹ 1 crore.In addition, over 240 Farmer Producer Organisation (FPO) start-ups are also being facilitated. The 900 to 1000 plus start-ups are being facilitated within a period of barely one year. This paper presents case illustrations of a few successful interventions catalysed in this perhaps very significant intervention in the developing world. Essentially, the paper validates an intervention approach that could efficiently complement the start-up initiative of the Government of India. It could also serve as a model for replication by related practitioners and institutions across the globe.

Entrepreneur: propeller behind the start-up

Evidently, the global fruit and vegetables processing industry is slated to have grown at an annual rate of 2.0 per cent over the last five years till 2016 and industry revenue is estimated at USD 274 billion. More importantly, the industry revenue is expected to expand at an annual rate of 3.0 per cent over the next few years till 2021, reaching USD 317.1 billion. Despite the potential, the agri business sector is yet to adequately mature in the country.There is tremendous scope to encourage entrepreneurship in this sector to both encourage value addition to the produce as well as generate employment.

Entrepreneurs may be viewed as individuals who explore opportunities, scan the environment, mobilise resources, convert ideas into viable business propositions and provide new products and services to society by bringing together and combining various factors of production. An "entrepreneurial" individual has a distinct vision and dream, which he/she is able to convert into products or services. As those of the "economists" genre will have it, an entrepreneur is a (planned) risk taker who effectively organises different factors of production. Such individuals are driven by tasks, challenges and opportunities and possess high level of achievement orientation.Basically, entrepreneurs are endowed with several qualities including- (i) need for achievement, (ii) perseverance, (iii) risk taking, (iv) preference for independence and "being one's own boss", (v) possess good inter-personal skills, (vi) possess a high degree of self-confidence, etc. It is this entrepreneur who facilitates start- ups albeit sustainably.Today, it is a widely accepted fact that entrepreneurs are not necessarily "born", but may also be created through training and exposure. Globally, there are several entrepreneurship development approaches. Nevertheless, a typical Entrepreneurship Development Programme (EDP) approach used by hundreds of institutions and non-governmental organisations (NGOs) in India adopts a mix of training and/or counselling/hand-holding interventions. The training interventions cover concepts and subjects like: (1) the "charm" of being an entrepreneur and basic entrepreneur qualities and traits, (2) methodology of opportunity identification and scanning the business environment, (3) methodology of business plan preparation and its assessment, and developing a perspective on the regulatory and supporting institutional and service provider framework, (4) basic management tools for successful operation and management of an enterprise. Along this vein, in many significantly agrarian economies like India, the agro and food processing sector offers vast scope for entrepreneurial initiatives. However, it is a commonly perceived fact that the success of different entrepreneurship development approaches has been limited and therefore there is a need for an integrated approach to be deployed to ensure start-ups in large numbers particularly in the labour and employment intensive MSE sector.

Indian agri business sector: an overview

India, with the second largest arable land in the world and diverse agro-climatic zones across the country, has significant production advantages in agriculture. Firstly, more than 52 per cent of India's land is cultivable, compared to the global average of 11 per cent. India produces 889.7 lakh tons of fruits and 1,628.9 lakh tons of vegetables. Also, it produces 62.3 lakh tons of meat and poultry, as well as 95.7 lakh tons of fish per annum. India has a wide variety of climate and soil on which a large range of horticultural crops such as fruits, vegetables and other tropical tuber crops, ornamental, medicinal and aromatic plants; plantation crops, spices, cashew and cocoa are grown.

The agri business and agro and food processing industry in the country is increasingly seen as a potential source for driving the rural economy as it facilitates synergy between industry and agriculture and promotes investment in the agricultural sector. India is also endowed with diverse agro-climatic conditions, around 46 soil types along with long sunshine hours and cropped area of 1,420 lakh hectares, which has helped the nation emerge as the largest producer of milk in the world, second largest producer of fruits and vegetables, third largest producer of food-grains and fish, and the largest number of livestock in the world. On the demand side, India offers a huge consumer base to the food industry with a population of 128 crore and increasing income levels.

Food and food products constitute the largest chunk of Indian consumer spending – about 46.5 per cent share of the consumers' rupee. Analysis of NSSO data indicated that the monthly per capita expenditure (MPCE) on food in India has grown at a CAGR of over 6 per cent in the last decade. The size of the food market is estimated to have grown at a CAGR of 7.86 per cent during this period. Presently, the size of the Indian food market is USD 300 billion.

During the last decade, India has seen dramatic changes in food consumption patterns. Analysis of data from the CSO indicates that the average national monthly per- capita expenditure on processed food has been rising over the years. Consequently, the share of cereals in consumer food expenditure has dropped from 33.8 per cent to 27.5 per cent over the decade. On the other hand, the share of processed food and beverages has increased from 8.5 per cent to 12.8 per cent, that of fruits and vegetables (F&V) has increased from 12.6 to 15.8 per cent and that of animal protein (egg, fish and meat) has increased from 5.4 per cent to 6.6 per cent. These trends signify that there is a consistent increase in the proportion of spending on high value categories such as beverages and processed food, F&V and processed meat products.

In the light of the above circumstance as well as resource and demand conditions vis-a-vis the agri-business sector, a range of micro and small enterprise start-ups have potential in the gamut of agro sub-sectors ranging from livestock farming to hatchery, poultry, pulses and cereals processing, carbonated beverages, spices processing, meat processing, fish processing, vegetable dehydration, fruit processing and warehousing to cold storage.

Agri business profile of Maharashtra and its constraints

On the basis of geographical features, the state of Maharashtra is divided into three natural regions: the Konkan comprising the coastal area; Sahyadri hill ranges (also known as western ghats); and the Deccan plateau. The major portion of the state is semi-arid with three distinct seasons of which the rainy season spreads over July to September. There are large variations in the quantity of rainfall within different parts of the state. The state has been divided into nine agro-climatic zones based on rainfall, soil type and the vegetation. While the agro and food processing sectors may be considered in terms of a number of sub-sectors:food crops, horticulture, plantation crops, spices and condiments, poultry, animal husbandry and fishery, the potential in terms of horticulture is particularly under-exploited. Maharashtra has the highest production of fruits in India. It is ranked first in grapes, pomegranate, banana and onion production and ranked second in papaya and sapota production. Maharashtra also ranks 9th in vegetable production with 5.6 per cent of India's total vegetable production.

With regard to fruit crops, Maharashtra is virtually the fruit bowl of the country. In the year 2013-14, the state had produced approximates. 134 lakh MT of fruits. The state has been ranked first amongst the Indian states accounting for 15 per cent of the overall fruit production of the country. The relative ranking of the state vis-à-vis the all-India production in case of fruits is depicted below.

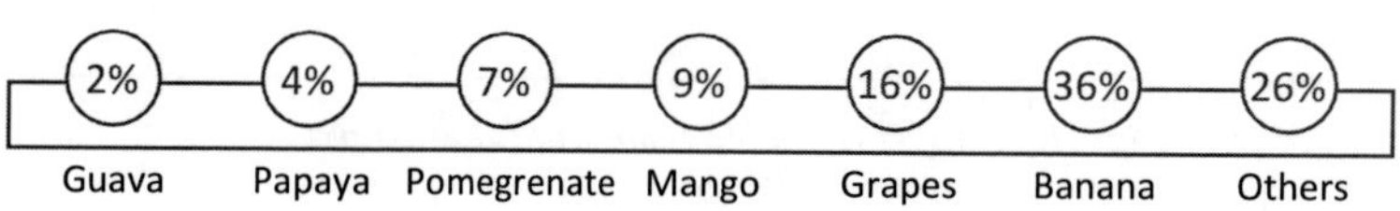

Fig. 11.1: Fruit crops in Maharastra

The key production centres are presented in the following table.

Table - 11.1: Concentration of major fruit crop production hubs in Maharashtra

Sl. No.	*Fruits*	*Production Hubs*
1.	Banana	Jalgaon, Hingloi, Nandurbar, Beed, Nanded, Pune, Ahmednagar, Kolhapur
2.	Lime/Lemon	Ahmednagar, West Solapur
3.	Mosambi	Aurangabad, Beed, Nanded

(*Contd...*)

4.	Orange	Amravati, Nagpur, Buldhana, Washim
5.	Grapes	Nashik, Solapur, Pune, Ahmednagar, Satara, Sangli
6.	Guava	Ahmednagar, Nashik, Satara, Beed, Pune, Aurangabad, Jalgaon
7.	Mango	Ratnagiri, Sindhudurg, Thane, Raigad, Aurangabad,Nanded, Latur, Hingoli
8.	Papaya	Ahmednagar, Pune, Nashik, Dhule, Jalgaon, Amravati
9.	Pomegranate	Solapur, Satara, Ahmednagar, Nashik, Pune, Sangli, Beed, Aurangabad
10.	Sapota	Thane, Pune, Ahmednagar

Source: Department of Agriculture and Co-operation, Maharashtra.

The state produced approximately. 101 lakh MT of vegetables in the year 2013-14. As against 2012-13, the production grew by approximately 27 per cent 2013-14. It was apparent that there was a marginal decline in 2012-13. However, the vegetable production rose again in 2013-14. The main vegetables produced in the State of Maharashtra are onion, tomato, cauliflower and brinjal. Statistics regarding the percentage share in state vegetable production is depicted below. Maharashtra is one of the major onion producing states in India. The crop is mainly cultivated in Nashik, Ahmednagar, Pune, Satara and Solapur. The relative ranking of the state vis-à-vis all- India production in case of vegetables is depicted below.

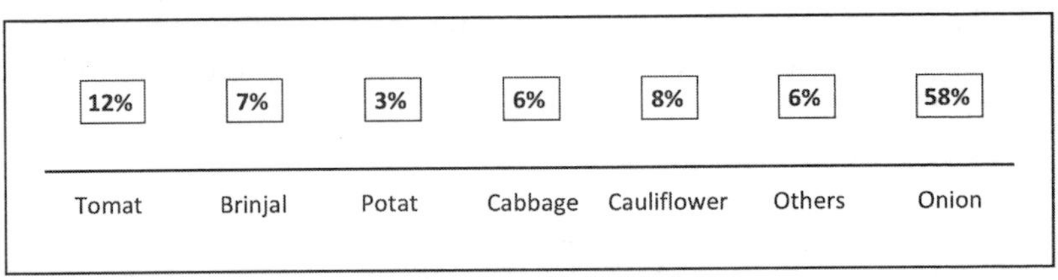

Fig. 11.2: Major vegetable crops of Maharashtra.

The key production centres in the state are captured in the following table:

Table - 11.2: Concentration of vegetable production hubs in districts of Maharashtra

Sl. No.	*Vegetables*	*Production centres*
1.	Brinjal	Nagpur, Satara, Solapur, Pune, Sangali, Dhule, Aurangabad, Beed, Nashik, Latur, Amravati
2.	Cabbage	Nashik, Pune, Satara, Nagpur, Ahmednagar, Sangli
3.	Cauliflower	Nashik, Satara, Pune, Nagpur, Ahmednagar, Beed
4.	Okra	Satara, Pune, Solapur, Jalgaon, Thane, Dhule, Nashik, Sangli

(*Contd...*)

5.	Onion	Nashik, Ahmednagar, Pune, Satara, Dhule, Jalgaon, Beed, Aurangabad, Latur, Nandurbar, Solapur
6.	Peas	Pune, Thane, Nandurbar
7.	Potato	Satara, Pune, Kolhapur, Ahmednagar
8.	Tomato	Nashik, Ahmednagar, Pune, Beed, Satara, Solapur, Latur, Nagpur

Source: Department of Agriculture and Co-operation.

Maharashtra's strength in the horticulture sector is apparent from the fact that it is the largest producer of seedless grapes, mandarin oranges, banana, tomato and onion. In fact, production of Alphonso mango in the state accounts for 75 per cent of India's export of mangoes. The state is a leader in the sugar milling industry with more than 150 co-operative sugar mills. The state also accounts for 40 per cent of total turnover of seed industry of the country. Export of fresh fruits and vegetables from Maharashtra accounts for 40 per cent of total export of F&V of the country. Export of processed food from Maharashtra accounts for 50 per cent of total exports from the country. The state houses more than 6,500 MSMEs and more than 300 large scale food processing industries. Diverse agro climatic conditions and various soil types add strength to the state horticulture sector in terms of seasonality and type of produce.

In spite of the strong raw material base and presence of large food processing units, the full potential of the sector is yet to be tapped as supporting farm proximate post- harvest infrastructure for horticultural crops is not fully developed. In fact, lack of processing and storage facilities and inefficient supply chain result in wastages (mainly in the form of value losses), estimated at 30 to 35 per cent in the case of fruits and vegetables. Some of the critical challenges faced by the horticulture sub-sector in the state are: inadequate farm proximate post-harvest infrastructure for handling and storage of food items/ perishables; relatively low level of processing. This implies the need for focusing on promotion of start-ups in related activities.

Entrepreneurship development approaches and ideal ED model

There is a range of approaches and strategies followed worldwide for entrepreneurship development. These include: (i) The group entrepreneurship and self-help group - SHG (and today even FPO led approach sometimes supported through micro audit and finance institutions or developmental or donor organisations). The success of the Bangladeshi "Grameen Bank" model of micro enterprise development through SHGs led to this approach being propagated and promoted in many countries. In India, the emerging success stories of the FPO led micro enterprise development model in locations such as Maharashtra under the Maharashtra Agricultural Competitiveness Programme (MACP) has led to this approach being propagated and promoted in many regions by the state governments in India, and the World Bank. (ii) The incubation centre and pilot plant approach has also been adopted by many agencies including the Ministries of Finance and Technology in India. (iii) The Entrepreneurship Development Programme (EDP) approach is also in practice, through which tens of thousands of trainees are trained every year in India alone. Such EDPs invariably involve offer of training inputs in entrepreneurship competencies, business opportunity identification, conduct of market survey, technical training in some cases, basic book keeping, business plan preparation, assistance (in some cases in securing loans). These EDPs are of 2 weeks to 3 months duration. However, many such EDPs (there certainly are exceptions) are seen to largely focus merely on success rate in "training" than in terms of number of candidates who actually start up enterprise operation. The latter varies from 10 to 30 per cent at best. Also, survival beyond the teething stage is often hardly even monitored. (iv) The approach involving the provision of mentoring services is undertaken by organisations such as the Youth Business International (YBI) head- quartered in the UK, and BharatiyaYuva Shakti Trust (BYST) which is India based. Some of them such as the BYST work closely with chambers /associations of existing enterprises (such as the Confederation of Indian Industry) whose members provide voluntary services in terms of mentoring support of 2 to 3 years for new entrepreneurs. However, apparently related initiatives have limitations in terms of limited number of start-ups, and scale of operation and interventions. It is in this circumstance that the search for ideal case illustrations of a few successful start-ups catalysed through this facility is captured in the following sections.

Case illustration on successful start-ups

Bhumata Food Products: targeting perceived local supply-demand gap

The town of Newasa in Ahmednagar district is located close to two holy places of repute, namely Shirdi and Shani Shinganapur. There are many restaurants and hotels in this town and nearby areas which require large quantities of spices and atta. At present, these eateries largely procure their inputs from spices processing units at far away Nagar and Aurangabad. Hence, the cost of procurement of spices for these hotels is high and logistics inconvenient. Upon identifying this need from the market and to exploit the local opportunity in the spices processing sector, an entrepreneur decided to establish an integrated food, and specifically spices processing unit. He is native to the region and this decided the locational choice of the project.

Being experienced in the line with more than 10 years of working in the food and pharma sectors, he was keen to set up an enterprise in his home town. He therefore approached the Agriculture Technology Management Agency (ATMA) office in the region, and requested and received training from the Krishi Vignan Kendra (KVK) in 2016 in spices processing. With the vision to grow and step into the food processing industry, the promoter has envisaged a plant for manufacturing various food products with the use of modern technology. This unit is today initiating production of various items such as coriander powder, cumin powder, chilli powder, turmeric powder and "Nachani Sattva".

Spices processing apparently has great market potential. As a matter of fact, India is renowned as the home for spices and boasts of a long history of spices trading with the ancient civilisations of Rome and China. Today, Indian spices are the most sought- after globally, given their exquisite aroma, texture, taste and medicinal value. India also offers the largest domestic market for spices in the world. As a matter of fact, India is the world's largest producer, consumer as well as exporter of spices. The country produces about 75 of the 109 varieties listed by the International Organization for Standardization (ISO) and accounts for one half of the global trading volume in spices. The country commands a formidable position in world spices trade with spice exports expected to touch about USD 3 billion by 2016-17. In value terms, India's spice market grows at an average of about 8.8 per cent per annum. About 8,93,920 tonnes of spices, valued at USD 2.4 billion were exported in 2014-15. The domestic and export market potential are both apparently very high.

After receiving training from theKVK, the entrepreneurwas offered guidance by the ABPF for the preparation of a bankable business plan for start-up of a project with outlay of ₹ 50 lakh in which ₹ 37.50 lakh was the loan component from the Bank of Baroda. This plan and project includes machinery like roasters, pulverisers, blenders, dryers and cleaning and packaging equipment. In addition to spices processing, the equipment can also process baby food like Nachani (finger millet) Sattva. The entrepreneur plans to deploy a unique marketing strategy using referrals from doctors to market Nachani Sattva.

In terms of manufacturing process, the promoter procures raw material from the weekly market as well as wholesale market at Ahmednagar.

He then dries it, and after drying, grinds it. Subsequently, depending upon the type of spice, blending activity is carried out. After blending, pouches of different sizes are packed. Considering 180 days of operation and on single shift basis, the projected turnover of the unit is ₹ 50 lakh per annum with direct employment generation for 22 workers (skilled and unskilled). The unit requires a large quantity of chilly, turmeric, coriander and finger millets. Therefore, in addition to business plan preparation for loan, the entrepreneur was guided on how he can competitively procure such inputs from FPOs in Ahmednagar and Aurangabad.

The promoter acclaims the ABPF as "a friend in need is a friend indeed". His request for loan has now been sanctioned and amount disbursed. Production has already been on in small scale. The entrepreneur is confident of successfully marketing his produce and growing his enterprise rapidly.

Ruchi Food Products: from household to commercial processing

SHG in India evolved with the global emergence of micro finance as the means for ensuring financial inclusion of the rural and urban poor in the developing nations. Notably, women played a prominent role in setting up and managing the SHGs. Presently, over 90 per cent of all the SHGs in India consist of women. Such SHGs are also seen as a platform for empowering women through financial inclusion. In this setting, near Pune city in the district of Pune, a woman entrepreneur formed a "Mahila Bachat Gat" with the intent of to promoting entrepreneurship amongst woman members, also of marketing the produce and encouraging their active participation in social welfare campaigns. This initiative led to the evolution of her own firm Ruchi Food Products in 2006 at Lohgaon (Pune). She started making pickles and chutneys on small scale, and members of the self-help group supported her in operating the enterprise.

The entrepreneur used to visit different food fairs and melas / exhibitions to sell her products, which she initially started manufacturing on household or cottage scale without the support of any bank loan. Soon she started receiving large orders for pickles and chutneys. In addition, customers and consumers often enquired on other products like karela, lemon and chilli pickles, flour items like ragi (finger millet) and papad, and so on. The entrepreneur therefore decided to expand and secure professional training in processing of various food products. She approached KVIC and professional training institutes for technical training in food processing.

Upon receiving technical training, the entrepreneur was assisted to prepare a bankable project report / business plan to set up a unit with project cost outlay of ₹ 99.67 lakh for availing loan from a bank. The entrepreneur approached the Canara Bank with the plan for realising a loan of ₹ 74 lakh (₹ 35 lakh as term loan and ₹ 39 lakh as working capital loan). The bank asked her to make several changes in the business plan as per their specific requirement. Team ABPF- Grant Thornton customised and re-casted the business plans three times over as per the modification suggested by the bank on scrutiny of the proposal prior to sanction. Her loan proposal to Canara Bank has now been effectively sanctioned.

Basically, the project comprises machinery and equipment like roasters, pulverisers, coating machine, oven, dryers and packaging equipment. The entrepreneur is expanding her enterprise capacity into larger commercial scale of operations using this equipment to exploit the ever growing market demand. Considering 300 days of operation on single shift basis, the projected turnover of the unit is ₹ 1.63 crore with direct employment generation for 10 to12 women (both skilled and unskilled). With current infrastructure and technology the unit was able to make an annual turnover of ₹ 67 lakh for the year 2015-16. GT-ABPF guided her on the options for raw material procurement from regional FPOs. The enterprise is also into Nachani (finger millet), raw mango and pulses. In addition, the entrepreneur has now approached exporters for marketing of such products abroad.

The promoter was also guided on different schemes in food processing for availing assistance by way of grant-in-aid. She is about to submit her proposal for added assistance under the SFAC scheme.

Kisan Agro Foods: from auto-rickshaws to carbonated soft drinks

Aurangabad is the capital of Marathwada and is virtually the tourism capital of Maharashtra. The city is a tourist hub, surrounded by many historical monuments, including the Ajanta and Ellora Caves, which are UNESCO World Heritage Sites. The region is also fairly industrialised with the presence of Bajaj Auto and Garaware Industries, which generate jobs for the skilled work force. Significantly, about 52.5 per cent of Aurangabad's population is in the 15–59 years age category implying a growing regional market for fast moving consumer goods (FMCGs) as well as for processed food. The promoter of this firm belongs to this city and was occupied as an auto rickshaw driver. He had the burning desire to start up his own business and be his own boss. He was fortunate to have the "peer" experience as his family was operating a small coconut water plant in Chennai and even marketing the produce in Mumbai. He availed of guidance from ABPF and prepared a plan which aims at producing carbonated soft drinks such as mango drinks, coconut water, guava juice and mixed fruit drinks. The entrepreneur's business idea had commonalities with his family's small coconut water processing project in Tamil Nadu. This is also in terms of distribution channels and aspects such as channel motivation strategies.

Market demand in the soft drink segment is apparently strong and growing. All - India production of aerated soft drinks is about 900 crore bottles per year, of which the production of carbonated soft drinks is about 70 per cent, that is, 630 crore bottles. Per capita consumption of carbonated drinks is about 4 bottles per year, which is low compared to other developing countries: Pakistan -13, Bangladesh-8, Egypt-3, and extremely low compared to USA where it is 350 bottles. Hence, there is considerable potential for consumption trends to rise. The market is apparently dominated by brands of leading pan-India companies such as Parle (46%), Pure Drinks (23%), McDowell (7%). Nevertheless, every Indian state has its own small local brands which have their own niche market. Typically, smaller firms and brands use customer push than consumer pull strategies to motivate marketing channels. Also, smaller firms basically offer higher margins to wholesalers and retailers.

The entrepreneur approached Vijaya Bank for realising the necessary loan, with the support of ABPF GT preparing a bankable plan. The start-up envisaged an outlay of ₹ 47.75 lakh of which ₹ 20 lakh is offered by the bank as term loan and ₹ 15 lakh for working capital. This project includes machinery like carbonator, water cleaning RO machine, filling machine, chiller, bottle mould, packaging equipment and printing cylinder. The entrepreneur is to target wholesalers and retailers to market his products.

In terms of manufacturing process in the facility, the first step is to purify water using an RO plant. The mixture of sugar, flavourings, essences, and water is called syrup. After water purification, such syrup clarification is an important step. Thereafter, carbonation (adding carbon dioxide to drink) takes place, followed by bottle filling. Considering 200 days of operation on conservative single shift basis, the projected turnover with current infrastructure, machinery and technology for the year 2015-16 was ₹ 12 lakh. The unit targets a turnover of ₹ 1.72 crore with direct employment generation for 8 workers (skilled and unskilled). The unit requires a large quantity of pomegranate, mango and guava. The ABPF guided the entrepreneur on how he can procure inputs from FPOs in Ahmednagar and Aurangabad districts.

Krushi Amrut Agro Food: from job-seeking to job-creating

An upcoming agri-business enterprise is located in Deolgaon Raja block of Buldhana district for processing amla and other products with modern equipment. This enterprise, to be well-equipped with machines and equipment, aims at production of various processed foods such as amla candy, amla powder, amla juice, etc. The enterprise Krushi Amrut Agro Foods is a proprietorship concern. The entrepreneur has acquired land for the project admeasuring 1,000 sq.ft. Bhalchandra is well qualified: a post-graduate diploma holder in Agricultural Extension Management from the National Institute of Agricultural Extension Management and B.Sc (Agriculture Bio-tech). The entrepreneur (along with other family members) has considerable exposure to food processing industry and has experience of more than 5 years in this line. As a matter of fact, the entrepreneur has also worked in the Agricultural Technology Management Agency (ATMA), Mahabaleshwar as subject expert for about three years. The enterprise is to manufacture value added products from amla, mango, jamun and tomato, and penetrate new markets in the Vidarbha region (including districts like Nagpur and Amravati).

Balachandra is an agriculture graduate who worked with the state agriculture department for about three years before deciding to move on to an entrepreneurial career. Amla, being available in sufficient quantity in the region and upon studying the increasing demand for amla products (also) in the light of its medicinal values, the entrepreneur decided to take up amla processing as an agri business option. Balachandra undertook detailed study for about 2 years which covered the aspects of raw material availability, machinery requirements, demand analysis, innovative product lines, etc. The entrepreneur also visited existing amla processing units in and around Buldhana to gain better understanding. After such detailed study the entrepreneur decided to take up entrepreneurship. After, a few months of running the business, the need for realising financial assistance arose. This is where ABPF-Grant Thornton played an important role. Experts from Grant Thornton prepared a techno commercial feasibility report taking into consideration the findings of the detailed study. The ABPF-GT team guided the entrepreneur on technical aspects such as innovative machinery, sources of raw material and packaging details. The entrepreneur was also made aware about various state and central government schemes which he can benefit from. Various licences such as FSSAI, NOC (No Objection Certificate)from Nagarpalika, Land NOC, Udyog Aadhar essential for the smooth functioning of business have been already secured.

In terms of manufacturing process, the raw material required is procured from nearby farmers and the local market place. Once the raw material, that is, amla, mango and plumis procured, they are vigorously washed so that the raw material is free of dirt and germs. The raw material is then boiled so that amla can easily be flaked or shredded. This amla is then dipped in concentrated sugar syrup to make amla candy. For amla juice, amla flakes are passed through a juice extractor and fresh amla concentrate is extracted. For making amla powder, amla flakes are completely dehydrated and then crushed to make fine powder. These products are then packed into various sizes with attractive labelling. The important machinery and equipment necessary for the proposed project is tray dryer, juice filling machine, bottle cap packing machine and an automatic packing machine. To consider the envisaged operations of the enterprise in detail, considering 252 days of operation on single shift basis, at 100 per cent capacity utilisation, enterprise operations will daily require 100 kgs of sugar, 500 gm. of preservatives (sodium benzoate), 1 LPG (fuel) cylinder (19 kg.), 250 grams of flavour and colours, 1 kg. salt and 1 kg. chat masala. The firm will also require packaging material like pet bottles and caps, packing wrappers, packing paper rolls, corrugated boxes, punch boxes (paper boxes), tape and big sized jars.

The total project cost amounts to about ₹ 31.46 lakh which is a mix of equity, grant from the NHM and loan to the tune of about ₹ 20 lakh from the Bank of India. As indicated, the entrepreneur has also applied for grant from Nation Horticulture Mission to the tune of ₹ 10.34 lakh and expects sanction from the Bank of India in a few days' time. The unit requires large quantity of amla, mango and plum and therefore the entrepreneur was guided on how he may procure this raw material from FPOs in and around Buldhana and other parts of Maharashtra. The projected turnover of the unit is about ₹ 3 crore per annum with direct employment generation to the tune of 10 workers (both skilled and unskilled).

The USP of Krushi Amrut Agro Foods is vis-à-vis originality of the ingredients maintained by avoiding use of preservatives. The products are free of synthetic colour and artificial flavour. Preservatives in minimum quantities are used only for amla juices. The critical success factor in this business is uniqueness of products; and there is almost no competition in similar products across the Vidarbha region. Furthermore, there is excellent availability of raw material and the cost of labour is also low in the region. The products manufactured by this entrepreneur are natural, healthy and are free of chemicals. Only basic preservatives are used in Amla juice, Mango juice and Jamun juice. The promoter is confident of successfully exploiting market potential and sustainably growing his enterprise.

Rujal Production: leveraging on demand for herbal and health food supplements

Rujal Production is a proprietary concern into the business of herbal product and health food supplement manufacture on micro scale, owned by a woman entrepreneur. She has established a small unit with own finance in District Pune, Maharashtra. The project is located in Lohegaon, Tal Haveli, Pune, Maharashtra, with built-up area admeasuring 1,500 sq.ft. The products being manufactured by the enterprise are amla, jamun, bittergourd, ashwagandha, shatawari and such powders as well as gulkand, shatawarikalp, chyavanprash, saunf (for household purposes), face pack, hair pack, mehendi, shikakai and hair oil. Entrepreneur Deepali is a diploma holder in electrical engineering and also owns an electronics firm. Importantly, she is trained in the field of manufacturing herbal products. She secured training inputs from the Khadi and Village Industries Commission.

The entrepreneur has always had a fascination towards herbal and health food supplement products and the likes to experiment with various herbal ingredients. Actually, she first started making products for personal use. Upon discovering positive results, she approached her relatives and neighbours with her products. These were highly appreciated by her relatives and friends and hence she started cottage or micro scale production of such products. By 2016, the entrepreneur decided to undertake production on larger commercial scale. She undertook a market survey by distributing samples of products and checked their acceptance. She also conducted a competitor analysis focusing on differentiating her products from competition. ABPF-GT helped the entrepreneur formalise her business through securing necessary statutory licences for starting and operating a business in the food processing sector in terms of Udyog Aadhar registration and Shop Act related licence. She has also registered for FSSAI licence and will be receiving the same soon. The USP of Rujal Production is purity, and self-concocted formulas of ingredients required to make various herbal and health food supplement products.

There has been a shift in the universal trend from synthetic to herbal medicines recently. It is ancient wisdom that plants have therapeutic value and are used to treat various diseases since the Neanderthal age. Apparently, all ancient civilisations in the world are known to use plants for medicinal purposes. Ayurveda and traditional Chinese medicines are well known to the world for their natural ingredients and multiple benefits. India has great potential as Mother Nature has bestowed the country with an enormous wealth of medicinal plants. India has often been referred to as the "Medicinal garden of the world". Today, people around the globe are giving preference to alternative medicines such as Ayurveda, naturopathy, homeopathy and herbal medicine. Demand for health food supplements is also on the rise. Growing awareness about medicinal benefits as well as therapeutic effect of herbal products is pushing up demand for herbal extracts, dietary supplements and herbal-based beauty aids worldwide. The demand scenario is therefore very positive.

The entrepreneur has adopted an intensive marketing strategy. She has fostered tie- ups with the majority of medical stores in and around Pune, especially medical stores in Lohegaon where the unit is established. The products are sold through Patanjali outlets under the Rujal Production brand. Door-to-door sales is another marketing strategy adopted by the entrepreneur and many sales personnel market products from door to door. Wholesale orders are also catered to by Rujal Productions. The products are marketed in various packet sizes such as 10gm., 50gm. and 100gm.

The total cost of the proposed project works out to ₹ 18,46,687. Out of this, the outlay on land and building is to the tune of ₹ 2,45,000. The necessary machinery and equipment component accounts for ₹ 8,20,155. Some of the other components of project cost include Preliminary & Pre-operative (P&P) expenses at about ₹ 1,50,000 and expense on furniture and fixtures to the tune of ₹ 50,000. The promoter also requires a working capital of ₹ 6,66,531 for the smooth functioning of the project. The project is to be established with a mix of equity and debt. Of the total project cost, promoter's contribution is pegged at about ₹ 4,61,672 which constitutes about 25 per cent of the total project cost, and term loan at ₹ 13,85,015 which amounts to 75 per cent of project cost. The project is expecting final sanction from the Canara Bank shortly.

The machinery the promoter is deploying for quality production is: Auto 15 kg. capacity roasting/mixing-cum-coating machine, single phase pulveriser machine, semi- automatic pouch packing machine, laminated paper and packaging machine. The manufacturing process of herbal products involves purchasing of raw material that is herbs, vegetables and fruits. These ingredients are then dried so as to make fine powder. Once they are dried properly, this raw material along with other essential ingredients is processed through a pulveriser to make a fine powder. This powder is then packed into different packet sizeswith proper labelling and is sold in the market through sales women. The enterprise is to be operated with a staff of about 15 women-force.

Samruddhi Agro Food Industries: from fertilisers to edible/non-edible oils

A proposed unit at District Ahmednagar, Maharashtra is a project moving to larger commercial scale of operations leveraging on debt finance. The entrepreneur has acquired land on a long term lease basis for 95 years from the MIDC in Shrirampur Industrial Area, Shrirampur taluka admeasuring 1,000 sq.metres. The proprietrix of this enterprise Samruddhi Agro Food Industries envisages investment in larger scale commercial production with modern equipment. The entrepreneur has envisaged a plant for manufacturing edible and non-edible oils from various types of oil seeds. To be well-equipped with machinery and equipment, this unit also exploits regional resource potential. The raw material (that is, groundnut, kardi, cotton, sunflower, castor, neem) used for preparation of various products will be used to produce edible as well as non-edible oils. This oil mill is to produce products like oil (ghani) and oil cake of flax seeds, cotton oil seeds and kardi seeds. Besides quality, another important factor to be laid emphasis on in this trade is packaging. This is in order to retain taste and nutritional value of products. Apparently, quality of the products has helped to garner the trust of clients of this proprietorship concern which has been in operation on micro or cottage scale for the last few months and has been involved in the extraction of edible and non-edible oils from oil seeds.

The entrepreneur along with other family members, has experience in the field of organic fertilisers and pesticides. Her spouse has 10 years experience of working in the manufacture of non-edible oil in Janki Agro Industries, Kolhar. The entrepreneur has a mission to process value added products from groundnut, kardi, cotton seed, sunflower, castor and neem in the light of absence of competition from other non- edible oil units in nearby areas, even while providing gainful employment to the local poor and providing forward linkages to local oil seeds and vegetable growers in the catchment area for inputs.

As a matter of fact, edible oil is one of the essential commodities used daily by the Indian populace for cooking purposes. Basically, edible oil is extracted from oil seeds like groundnut, kardi, cotton, sesame, linseed, mustard, rape seed and sunflower. Non- edible oil is used for medicinal purposes, in soaps and lubricants, and can be extracted from commodities like castor and neem. for the extraction of the oil, oil "ghanis" are typically used. For greater commercial production in larger units expellers are deployed. Traditionally, oil ghanis were manned by bullocks. However, today they are operated by power (electricity). Power ghanis may be found in both rural and urban areas. Oilseeds and edible oils are two of the most sensitive agricultural commodities in the country. Moreover, India contributes to about 9 per cent of the world oilseeds production, to about 7 per cent of the global production of protein meal, and is the fourth largest edible oil economy in the world. The supply and demand base are both strong. Within the country, Madhya Pradesh is the leading oilseed producing state accounting for about 21 per cent of total oilseed production. The other leading oilseed producing states are Gujarat, Rajasthan, Maharashtra and Andhra Pradesh. Oilseeds, edible and non-edible oil play an important role in the agricultural economy of the country. Groundnut, rapeseed, mustard, soybean, sunflower, sesame, niger seed, castor and linseed are the nine major sources for obtaining edible and non-edible grade oils. In this regard, the secondary sources comprise coconut, cottonseed and rice bran solvent extracted oils of tree and forest origin.

The entrepreneur's spouse who is partly supporting her entrepreneurial venture has a farming background. Being aware of the demand potential for neem he decided to establish facilities to process neem into neem oil. Apparently, the idea of processing neem to produce neem oil struck in his mind even when he was pursuing his graduation studies. The husband and wife team undertook extensive market research for a couple of years. They deeply studied the manufacturing process, raw material requirement, as well as machinery requirement for running the business. The entrepreneur also carried out a SWOT analysis which highlighted that own funds alone were not sufficient for setting up a related enterprise and hence decided to seek financial assistance from their bankers, the Canara Bank. Upon approaching the bank with a rough business plan they were advised to prepare a detailed project report or business plan with projected balance sheets, P&L statement, cash flows as well as indicators of financial viability. The entrepreneur was guided on technical aspects such as necessary machinery, sources of raw material and packaging options, also enlightened about various state and central government schemes of assistance, on the regulatory compliances vis-à-vis FSSAI, pollution control and Udhyog Aadhar. NOC from the MIDC has been already acquired.

The promoter procures raw material from farmers in the nearby locality. They are crushed finely and oil extracted with the help of extraction equipment. The product is then filtered, leaving behind oil and fat based residue. The oil extracted is then packed into various package sizes, while the fat based residue is used in soap industry as raw material. Apart from fat residue, the residue of crushed seeds is also obtained. This seed residue is passed through a pulveriser and moulded into fine cakes which is an excellent cattle feed. The oil cakes are in great demand as consumption of these cakes by cattle increases milk capacity. Therefore, the various products that may be manufactured from oil seeds including oil, fat based residue and oil cakes all have considerable demand. The machinery and equipment being deployed for the project comprise oil expeller, boiler, pulveriser filter press, conveyors, weighing machine and stitching machines. In terms of project revenues, considering 300 days of operation on single shift basis, the projected turnover of the unit is ₹ 4.6 crore with direct employment generation for 8 workers (skilled and unskilled) initially. Notably, this business activity requires edible and non-edible oil seeds such as sunflower, safflower, caster, kardi and neem. in large quantities, acquired directly procurement from farmer producer companies based in and around Ahmednagar district. The enterprise has realised assistance by way of debt capital to the tune of ₹ 22 lakh from the Canara Bank and is well into project implementation.

Shrinath Food Products: case of convenience food wheat processing

A convenience food processing unit is in operation in District Ahmednagar, Maharashtra. The project is set up in Mhase, Tal-Shrigonda, Ahmednagar in area admeasuring 2,400 sq.ft. Convenience food products are growing in demand. In today's era of women working to eke out a living, there is ever increasing demand for such foods. An enterprise coming up in Ahmednagar caters to this need in a changing society and seeks to manufacture wheat flour. The enterprise is to manufacture readymade wheat flour in various packet sizes for easy consumption. The firm Shrinath Food Products is a proprietary concern. That has successfully commenced operations in 2016.

Before commencing operations initially on cottage/micro scale sans institutional credit, the promoter undertook trial production and processed wheat flour in small quantities. The entrepreneur checked the quality of flour as well as its physical appearance and tested its acceptability in the market. Prior to commencing the operations, the entrepreneur visited the existing wheat flour mills for gaining practical knowledge. The raw material required for processing is wheat, procured from farmers in that area. Thereafter, he observed that his own funds alone were not sufficient for setting up the business unit and hence he opted for financial assistance from the Central Bank. In this regard, the promoter was guided on related equipment and technology, input sourcing and on packaging, as also on aspects such as FSSAI, lab testing reports and securing NOC from the Gram Panchayat. Importantly, the entrepreneur believes in purity and in maintaining the quality of the product which is already fetching him good business. Apparently, unlike flour from many other manufacturers, his product is free of any adulteration and impurities. The entrepreneur uses a special Marshal atta chakki that helps in retaining the originality and maintaining quality of wheat flour. The demand for branded cereal flour products is now increasing. Even big giants like Hindustan Lever, NEPC Agro and Nirma have jumped into this lucrative industry. Wheat flour is predominantly used in food items in India, such as chapatti, roti, naan and puri, and in sweet items too like in halwa and pakoda. Owing to the public distribution system providing whole wheat which has to be grounded and also purchasing wheat from the open market and grinding it, it will be cheaper than flour available in the market and one has the option to grind it to the consistency required. These advantages generate a huge market potential for a mini wheat flour mill. A simple low cost mini wheat mill is ofgreat relevance especially in rural regions. It can produce common milled wheat products in small quantities at a low investment.

The enterprise procures raw material (wheat) from traders from Madhya Pradesh and also from the local market. After procuring wheat, it is cleaned through use of destoner and pre-cleaner and then sieved so as to remove the stones and husk, if any. This cleaned wheat is then processed through a flour mill until fine powder of desired quality is obtained. This flour is now packed into various packet sizes. The enterprise caters to both retail and wholesale market. Major buyers of wheat flour are households, retail units, hotels, hospitals and catering businesses. Considering 180 days of operation on single shift basis, the projected turnover of the unit is ₹ 58.80 lakh with employment generation for 6 workers (skilled and unskilled), initially. The total project cost for this enterprise is 8.98 lakh which is a mix of both equity and bank loan. The entrepreneur's contribution has been in the range of 2.24 lakh (25%), and the balance bank loan.

Today, the entrepreneur is exploring the option of procuring input wheat from FPOs in the region, and to manufacture protein flour which has good demand. Such flour is recommended by doctors to overcome deficiency of proteins - essential to repairing wear and tear activities in the human body.

Dayanand Agro Foods: from primary cleaning and grading to flour milling

Indian producers are unable to realise optimal value from their produce mostly due to fragmented land holdings and inability to reap scale economies enjoyed by large farms. India has over 12.5 crore farmer households, of which over 85 per cent are small and marginal farmers with land holdings of less than 2 hectares each and at barely 1.33 hectares per farmer household. Typical small and marginal farmers cannot gain efficiencies from quantity procurement of inputs, or deploy costly farm and post-harvest technologies. Such had been the situation of the farmers in Phulambri taluka of Aurangabad district. Around 50 per cent of farmers in this region go in for distress sale of their produce in order to service credit availed for agro input purchase and domestic requirements. They sell their produce to traders in the local mandis only. They have limited exposure to other markets or sales channels. They submit to the dictates of local traders due to the inability to scout and link with other potential buyers and suffer from unfavourable trading terms. The farmer producer company (FPC) as an institution evolved as a silver lining for such farmers, as it has helped them utilise scale to procure inputs at a lower price and achieve more bargaining power while marketing their products. It has also helped them access timely and adequate finance, build capacity and gain direct linkages to markets. In view of this, and as per the mandate of the Maharashtra Agricultural Competitiveness Project (MACP), farmers from 9 villages came together and formed the Dayanand Agro Producer Company which has successfully implemented a common facility centre for primary processing of agri inputs with MACP assistance.

Alongside, one of the directors of Dayanand Agro Producer Company decided to start an independent wheat flour milling and packaging unit in order to cater to the needs and demands of local farmers associated with the FPC. This flour unit is to support the demand and supply from around 2,360 households (HHs) and 5,801 hectares of cultivable land in the region. The unit has been set up in an area measuring 1,500 sq. ft. at Jalgaon, located in the taluka Phulambri of Aurangabad district, Maharashtra. The related processing plant has the capacity to process 20 quintals of wheat per hour. The enterprise is to operate for 8 hours a day, processing around 14.4 tonnes of produce at 90 per cent efficiency. This capacity allows the processing unit to mill only a small proportion of total grain production in the region. Mete was offered guidance for the preparation of a bankable plan by ABPF-GT to start up a project with an outlay of ₹ 121.95 lakh, of which ₹ 30.48 lakh was the term loan component from the Canara bank. This plan and project includes the wheat cleaning machine, gravity separator, wheat crusher, flour mill, packing machine and other accessories. The project is expecting the sanction soon but operation has already been initiated in smaller cottage scale by the promoter.

In terms of manufacturing process, the enterprise is to procure raw wheat grains directly from the FPC as well as from other farmers. This is then cleaned and milled. Subsequently, depending upon the type of output, refined wheat flour, rawa, maida (75%) and mill feed (25%) are obtained. Considering 240 days of operation on single shift basis, the projected turnover of the unit is ₹ 780 lakh with direct employment generation for 8 workers (skilled and unskilled).

The promoter has extensively researched the challenges and opportunities in marketing of agro products in the district and other major markets. In fact, the packaged wheat flour market in India started breaking the age-old tradition of grinding wheat at local chakki by growing at a whopping compound annual growth rate (CAGR) of 19 per cent. The wheat flour market was largely dominated by local chakkis in India. However, the branded packaged wheat flour segment is emerging rapidly in the country by offering better quality, nutrition and convenience. As indicated, Dayanand Agro Foods has started selling its branded packaged wheat flour in small scale in the local market of Ahmednagar. The promoter looks forward to expanding the processing capacity of the four mill to larger commercial scale in the near future with debt finance and thereafter even extend the product line as the business grows.

Pundlik Baba Rice Mill: Whole family involved rice milling start-up

Bhandara is a rather small district in the state of Maharashtra and the fifth least populated. About 80 per cent of the populace live in rural areas, and agriculture occupies an important place in the rural economy of the district. In the light of soil composition and rain fall, paddy is the major crop grown in the district along with other crops such as wheat, tur, gram, turmeric and linseed. Out of the total 3,89,000 hectares of geographical area, the total area under cultivation is 2,64,000 hectares. The total area under paddy is about 1,74,000 hectares. Hence, paddy is the major crop in kharif season - over 2,00,000 farmers in the district are directly involved in paddy cultivation. As a matter of fact, Bhandara is also popularly referred to as the "Rice Bowl of Maharashtra". Finest quality rice is being regularly exported from Bhandara and nearby regions to the quantum of over 29,000 TEUs (Twenty-foot Equivalent Units) annually via the road route of NH-6 through CONCOR's Inland Container Depot at Ajni, Nagpur to countries like South Africa and parts of Russia. There are over 243 registered rice mills (mostly micro scale) and many rice brokers and agents in the district. The district basically enjoys convenient availability of raw material paddy, good connectivity logistically and a large number of related and supporting service providers.

The entrepreneur and her family have extensive experience of paddy farming and years of experience in rice milling (through their micro-sized enterprise - Harde Rice Mill). As a matter of fact, the Hardes are a farmer family turned first generation entrepreneurs, who have continued their occupation of paddy farming as well as ventured into rice milling. Upon understanding the services of ABPF-GT team, Kunda Harde and her son approached the team for assistance. Her ward, Harshwardhan Harde, thereon worked closely with ABPF-GT. Though the promoters sought to establish a modern integrated rice mill, machines like whiteners and silky polishers are rather capital intensive. The promoters decided on a simple (khauti type) rice mill where job work could be pursued. In a khauti type mill basic custom milling of paddy to rice conversion is facilitated. Such mill, however, does not include machines like whiteners and silky polishers. In the absence of such machines, the finished product is not marketable and is generally further processed by upgraded or modern mills for final marketable finished products. The team guided the promoters on schemes like CLCSS, SFAC Venture Capital Assistance Scheme, MAIDC's NMFP scheme and PSI 2013. After having understood how the combination of some of these schemes would considerably lower their liability in future, the promoters decided to go in for a modern integrated project. The plan envisages production of polished rice and by-products like bran and husk.

The promoters were offered support for the preparation of a bankable business plan by ABPF-Grant Thornton for the project with project cost of ₹ 76.19 lakh in which ₹ 30 lakh is offered by the bank as term loan, ₹ 9.53 lakh is envisaged under SFAC venture capital assistance and the balance being contributed by the promoters. The enterprise is also eligible for subsidy of 25 per cent on project cost under the NMF scheme of the MAIDC. The promoters are bringing in the amount equivalent to subsidy till the time the amount is received from government agencies. Further, about ₹ 25 lakh is required from the bank as working capital. This project includes machinery and equipment like pre-cleaner, de-stoner, de-husker, paddy separator, whiteners and silky polisher. The promoters target selling the products through commission agents, wholesalers and retailers. The promoter family has experience of many years in the food grain business and has an established network across Bhandara and other regions of the country.

The manufacturing process in the upcoming facility basically involves warehousing (storage), pre-cleaning and de-stoning, de-husking, paddy separation, thickness grading, whitening, polishing, length grading and packaging. Considering average (over) 200 days of operation on single shift basis, the projected turnover of the unit is 4.29 crore with direct employment generation for 28 workers (skilled and unskilled). The unit is expected to also partly source its paddy requirements from FPOs in Bhandara, Gondia, Chandrapur and Gadchiroli districts. The promoters request for loan has been recently sanctioned by the Bank of Maharashtra.

Sulabh Industries: Dal milling in the orange city

Nagpur is the winter capital and the third largest city of the Indian state of Maharashtra and the largest city of central India. The city has many features in its favour. It has been adjudged as the 20th cleanest city in India and the top mover in the western zone as per Swachh Sarvekshan 2016. Nagpur is reputed as the "Tiger Capital of India" as it connects many tiger reserves in India to the world. It is among the important cities for the information technology sector in Maharashtra. The city is located in the centre of the country with the Zero Mile marker indicating the geographical centre of India. In terms of the agri-business sector, Nagpur is famous for the "Nagpur Orange" and is reputed as the "Orange City" for being a major trade centre of oranges cultivated in the region. Nagpur is also home to ice-cream manufacturer Dinshaws, Indian dry food manufacturer Haldiram's, Indian ready-to-cook food manufacturer Actchawa and Ayurvedic products companies Vicco and Baidyanath. Owing to the large production of pulses in the region (in Nagpur, Amravati and Yavatmal), dal milling has been one of the important sectors for investment for many entrepreneurs. As a matter of fact, the Dall Mill Cluster of Nagpur is a large cluster and is in the process of commissioning a large modern Common Facility Centre with assistance under the MSECDP scheme of Ministry of MSME.

An entrepreneur and her family members are part of the dal milling fraternity and been in the dal mill business for many years now and have vast experience in the industry. The promoter is one of the leading and reputed manufacturers of pulses in Nagpur. Huge demand for its processed pulses and need for automation prompted the promoters to expand and upgrade the existing plant. The promoters understood the gamut of services provided under the ABPF including backward linkages with the region's FPOs and farmer groups. Being in industry for years, they understood the importance of such activity to ensure effective procurement of raw material. Madhuri's son Sulabh Gupta availed of guidance of ABPF-Grant Thornton team and prepared a plan which aims at production of pulses, by-products like chunni, bhusi and khanda.

He approached the Union Bank with a bankable plan prepared by ABPF-Grant Thornton for a project outlay of ₹ 62.50 lakh, of which ₹ 15 lakh is term loan by the bank, ₹ 6.50 lakh is interest free loan envisaged under the SFAC Venture Capital Fund, ₹ 15.50 lakh envisaged as grant from MoFPI and ₹ 25.50 lakh contributed by the promoter. This project includes machinery like de-stoner, classifier (with aspirator), dryers, rolls and electric panels. The entrepreneur targets selling the products through commission agents, wholesalers and retailers. The promoter family has experience of many years in the food-grain business, and hence has established a strong connection with consumers across Bhandara and other regions of the country.

The manufacturing process involves: cleaning, grading, de-stoning and then drying, grading, de-husking, splitting, colour sorting, polishing and packaging. Considering 300 days of operation on double shift basis, the projected turnover of the unit is ₹ 24.29 crore with direct employment generation for 12 workers (skilled and unskilled). The unit requires large quantity of pulses as inputs and hopes to procure it from FPOs in Amravati, Yavatmal and other districts. The promoters' request for loan has now been sanctioned and the project is being implemented in right earnest.

Concluding note

The case studies presented in this paper offer insights into a range of business opportunities in the agro and food processing sector. They also present a wide canvas of entrepreneur typologies.

Most entrepreneurs had leaped into their entrepreneurial career as a "positive pull" than a "negative push". Many are well qualified and some have even involved with the government before. Products manufactured by the entrepreneurs vary from rice and pulses, pickles and chutney, to carbonated soft drinks, neem oil, amla powder and juice, wheat flour to edible oil exploring a wide range of local resources.

The promoters have benefited from technical training inputs by organisations like ATM, KVK and the DIC, and have inverted in projects with loans from banks to the turnover of ₹ 10 to 20 lakh. The entrepreneur has used a wide range of promotional strategies ranging from referral from doctors to marketing through SHGs. These smaller firms have withstood and are, successfully competing in the market using a "customer push" than "consumer pull" based marketing strategy. A range of financial institutions have supported their debt financing requirements albeit with necessary collateral.

In essence, the integrated EDP approach largely involved selection of (technically) trained candidates and thereafter providing business plan related orientation and inputs over several individual sittings with concerned entrepreneurs by the ABPF. Inputs were provided vis-a vis technology choice marketing strategy and credit options amongst others. Some of the start-ups have also evolved from SHGs and FPOs. The ABPF also facilitated business plan preparation and sanction of loan followed by basic vectoring services over the teething stage. Numerous "start-up and stakeholder meets" complemented the entrepreneur selection and linkage aspects. FPOs comprising small and marginal farmers are also being benefitted over the intervention by means of serving as sourcing hubs. The cases basically validate the approach requiring dedicated hand-holding services for business plan preparation, loan syndication and mentoring for technically trained or even EDP trained candidates to ensure large scale start-ups in the MSME sector.

12

CHALLENGES TO RURAL ENTREPRENEURSHIP DEVELOPMENT IN ASSAM: AN EMPIRICAL STUDY

DIPANJAN CHAKRABORTY
POM SEN CHAKRABORTY

Abstract

India lives in villages, which becomes obvious from the fact that more than 7,200 lakh of its population lives in about 6 lakh villages of this country. But even after 60 years of independence, rural India is characterised by severe poverty, illiteracy, lack of health services, lack of employment opportunities and overall backwardness. Entrepreneurship is a complex and multi-faceted phenomenon. The share of agriculture has increasingly declined in recent years resulting in continuous migration to urban areas in search of better employment opportunities and living standards. Hence, there is need to strengthen employment opportunities in the rural areas by promoting rural entrepreneurship. The study is made in the Sonitpur district of Assam, based on data collected from 100 rural micro entrepreneurs through interview schedule. The findings suggest that most of the entrepreneurs face problems of marketing, managerial, financial, environmental, control and evaluation, etc. The paper concludes with a few suggestions based on the findings.
Keywords: *Entrepreneurship, rural entrepreneurship, micro entrepreneurs.*

Introduction

India lives in her villages'- this axiom is true even today despite the service sector budding in the urban and semi-urban areas. But there is a large area of darkness in the rural hinterland. About 7,200 lakh people live in 6 lakh villages of India. Of the total work-force, 60 per cent are engaged in agriculture. The contribution of agriculture to GDP is merely 16 per cent (Singh and Namboodiri 2006). Any progress of growth and development that does not fulfill the needs of rural area and its people, especially the poor, cannot be claimed as development (Sinha 2010). Therefore, to strengthen the economy there is a need to develop the villages. For development of rural economy, India needs the foundation of industrialisation in the rural area, ensuring the utilisation of existing resources and exploring the various hidden potentialities (Sinha 2010). India's north-east region is poised for a major economic leap along with the rest of the country. The development of rural entrepreneurship is considered to be a panacea for harnessing vast untapped human resource in this region. Rural progress must ultimately depend on industrialisation. It can be said that growth of rural India can only be supported by the growth of rural entrepreneurship, which alone has the unique capacity of creating jobs through the successful emergence of small and micro ventures (Santana and Jegadeesan 2008).

Statement of problem

The growing intensity of international competition and globalisation is affecting the growth of micro enterprises in the developing economies. Among the various difficulties of micro enterprises, lack of smooth supply of raw materials and working premises were reported to be the major bottlenecks facing the small scale manufacturing industries, while lack of sufficient capital and working premises were the leading problems of the informal sector operators in starting their businesses. In Assam, since there have not been any organised policy and support systems that cater to the sector, micro enterprises have been confronted by various problems of policy, of structural and institutional nature. The existing business associations are financially weak and most of them have a very limited capacity to actually support and strengthen their members. Most of the rural micro enterprises have not yet been embraced by the existing business associations and chambers, thus excluded from any form of support that could be obtained from them. And hence in this study the major problems of rural micro enterprises will be identified and recommendations will be given.

Literature review

Hossain and Uddin (2006), in their study on Problems in Financing and Managing Small-Scale Enterprises in Bangladesh, found that inadequate amount of loan, excessive formalities in loan processing, high interest rate and loan processing cost, unfavourable repayment policy and absence of financial institutions in rural areas are main problems in financing. The operating problems are inadequate infrastructure, inefficient marketing facilities and market information, lack of proper training and skilled workers, lack of proper R&D facilities, outdated technology and technical know-how, etc. Solving these problems is important for proper development of SSEs through state intervention, social and political institutions that will ensure economic development of the country.

Ramalaingam and Gayatri (2006) suggest using innovation as a strategic tool for the development of rural entrepreneurship. Since most of the Indian population live in rural villages, entrepreneurship awareness has to be created among them. The multi- dimensional aspects of rural entrepreneurship are studied with the help of a small size sample. The findings suggest that a small innovation in the rural area would definitely catch up with most of the population that would lead to improvement of quality of life of many people in the country.

Geetha and Govindappa (2011) made a study on socio-economic background and problems of entrepreneurs in the industrial estate in Davangere district of Karnataka. The study found that entrepreneurs faced different kinds of operational problems with respect to raw material, marketing, power, finance, technical and managerial assistance in running their units. The study suggests that industrial estates have to be properly coordinated with the broader development programme.

Dey and Rahman (2010) in their study on micro and small enterprises in two hill districts of Assam, viz, Karbi Anlong and North Cachar hills, found that micro and small enterprises of Assam hills suffered from several inherent problems which stand in the way of spontaneous growth. Industrial development in Assam hills has not reached the desired extent due to inadequate infrastructure facilities, lack of entrepreneurial class and unfavourable socio-economic conditions.

Khanka (2009) conducted a survey of 248 first generation entrepreneurs in Assam to understand their entrepreneurial motivation. The study clearly showed that the entrepreneurs were primarily motivated by the need for economic achievement, personal growth, autonomy and recognition. The desire to contribute to the community was not found to be an important reason to become an entrepreneur. The study did not reveal any significant difference in the motivations of male and female entrepreneurs.

Kumar and Lalhunthara (2012) in their study on socio-economic background of micro entrepreneurs in Aizawl district, Mizoram found that education, experience, age and family play an important role in shaping the entrepreneurial ambition of the aspirant. It was found that nearly 25 per cent of entrepreneurs were females. Their study also revealed that entrepreneurs were engaged in different lines of business activities ranging from tailoring to food processing, involving complex technologies and different skill sets.

Objectives of the study

The overall objective of the study is to examine the general problems of rural micro enterprises and to give recommendation for the problems identified. The specific objectives are:

To identify problems with regard to finance, marketing, management and HRM, infrastructure, etc.

To forward possible suggestions and strategies to solve the problems.

Methodology

To achieve the aforementioned objective, the researcher has collected and reviewed relevant documents and information from both secondary and primary sources. The secondary data sources include pertinent documents, published and unpublished. The primary data were obtained from rural micro enterprises registered with DIC, Tezpur through questionnaire from 10 different blocks selected at random by convenient sampling method; 160 questionnaires were distributed in the 10 blocks, and only 120 were returned, of which only 100 were relevant. The data collected was analysed through manual and computerised systems. The study covers a period of two years, 2014-15 and 2015-16.

Data analysis, interpretation and findings

The objective of the study was to investigate critical factors affecting the performance and development of rural micro enterprises in Sonitpur district. Data was collected from 100 micro enterprises operating in the rural area of Sonitpur district through questionnaire during the reference period, and analysed using descriptive statistics.

Critical problems/ analysis

The questionnaire contained 35 items (factors) and the respondents were asked to evaluate the problems that had impact on the performance of rural micro enterprises on a scale ranging from strongly agree to strongly disagree and "I don't know". Since it is difficult to analyse and compare these 35 items, it is important to group them into manageable number of problem categories. The 35 items were originally developed under six theoretical categories: Environmental, Managerial, Marketing, Financial, Control and Evaluation factors. Each factor has five to eight lists of problems/factors.

Environmental factors

Micro enterprises are facing challenges due to changes in social, cultural, economical, technological, demographic changes and political-legal environment. Technology changes the way micro enterprises are doing business. New technology is usually expected to reduce the cost of product or service.

Table - 12.1: Environmental factors

S/N	*Environmental factors*	*Agree*	*Disagree*	*I don't know*	*Missing*
1.	Intensity of competition	67 (67%)	20 (20%)	13 (13%)	---
2.	Availability/affordability of business licence	48 (48.5%)	42 (42.4%)	9 (9.1)	1
3.	Rapid and costly technological changes	51 (52.0%)	29 (29.6%)	18 (18.4%)	2
4.	Climate conditions	38 (38%)	33 (33%)	29 (29%)	
5.	Bureaucracy in company registration & licensing	43 (43%)	40 (40%)	17 (17%)	
6.	Lack of government encouraging policy	39 (39.4%)	47 (47.4%)	13 (13.1%)	1
7.	The impact of national culture: values, norms	41 (41.4%)	47 (47.4%)	11 (11.1%)	1
8.	Inability to compete with other firms/products	32 (32%)	41 (41%)	27 (27%)	

Source: Field survey.

The above table shows that the environmental factors affect the performance of micro enterprises. As shown, the respondents agreed on the five problems from the eight lists. And the result shows that 67 per cent agreed on the intensity of competition (only 20% disagree), 48.5 per cent agree on the availability/affordability of business licence (42.4% disagree), 52 per cent agreed on rapid and costly technological changes (29.6% disagree), 38 per cent agreed on climate conditions and 43 per cent agreed on bureaucracy in company registration and licensing (40% disagree). Most of the respondents disagreed on the other three problems of culture, norms and values.

Marketing factors

Micro and small enterprises in India are facing increasing difficulties in marketing their products/services and generally are not utilising their production capacity to the fullest extent for the same reason. Permal in his study "Rural entrepreneurship and rural employment" observed that rural entrepreneurs are not able to reach the market themselves and thus middlemen were making huge profits. Some of the recent studies found that the small entrepreneurs are yet to realise the importance of marketing and adopt modern marketing techniques.

Table - 12.2: Marketing factors

S/N	*Marketing factors*	*Agree*	*Disagree*	*I don't know*	*Missing*
1.	Lack of skill to set clear competitive pricing policy	54(54%)	39(39%)	7(7%)	
2.	Lack of demand	52(52%)	44(44%)	4(4%)	
3.	Lack of marketing knowledge	46(46%)	38(38%)	16(16%)	
4.	Poor quality packaging	51(49.1%)	48(50.9%)	-	1
5.	Poor customer relationship & handling	44(44%)	56(56%)		

Source: Field survey.

As shown in table-12.2, lack of skill to set clear and competitive pricing policy was the most critical problem on which 54 per cent of the respondents agreed and 52 per cent agreed that lack of demand and supply forecasting is another problem; 46 per cent of the respondents agreed on lack of knowledge of market, 51 per cent agreed on poor quality of packaging, while 56 per cent disagreed on poor customer relationship and handling.

Financial factors

Finance is one of the main components for entrepreneurial growth. This is particularly true of micro and small enterprises where the role played by capital is relatively important. The performance of micro enterprises is affected by lack of financial record keeping and documentation, insufficient provision for contingencies, high investment in fixed assets, high interest rates charged by banks, too many formalities of banks, harsh and hard repayment schedule, inadequately estimated capital requirements, inability to analyse financial statements.

Table - 12.3: Financial factors

Sl. No.	*Financial factors*	*Agree*	*Disagree*	*I don't know*	*Missing*
1	Inadequacy and costly of credit facilities and sources	63(62.6%)	33(33.3%)	3(3.0%)	1
2	Shortage of working capital	61(61%)	34(34%)	5(5%)	
3	High investment in fixed assets during start-up time	58(58%)	38(38%)	4(4%)	
4	Lack of record keeping	46(46%)	39(39%)	15(15%)	
5	Failure to analyse f/statements	52(53.1%)	41(41.8%)	5(5.1%)	2
6	Harsh and hard repayment schedule	48(48.5%)	50(50.5%)	1(1.0%)	1
7	Too many formalities of banks	58(58%)	40(40%)	2(2%)	
8	High rates of interest	57(57.6%)	38(38.4%)	4(4.0%)	1

Source: Field survey.

The major contributors to this factor, as indicated in table-12.3, are the inadequacy and costly credit facilities and sources (62.6% agree), Shortage of working capital (61% agree), high investment in fixed assets during start-up time (58% agree), lack of record keeping and documentation (46% agree), failure to analyse financial statements (53% agree), harsh and hard repayment schedule, (48.5% agree), too many formalities at banks (58% agree), high rates of interest (57.6% agree). About 50.5 per cent of the respondents disagreed on harsh and hard repayment schedule being a problem. According to the weight and magnitude of the problems, it is clear that all the factors played a significant role in obtaining finance towards the establishment and expansion of their business.

Managerial & HRM factors

Many researchers and practitioners claim that the major cause of small business failure is "poor management". Whether or not the causes are labelled as financing, competition, marketing, inventory, etc., they can be safely avoided if good management is in place. If they are to succeed, managers need to have adequate skills in the area of planning, organising, directing and controlling organisational resources.

Table - 12.4: Managerial & HRM factors

S/N	*Managerial & HRM factors*	*Agree*	*Disagree*	*I don't know*	*Missing*
1.	Lack of strategic business planning	60(52.2%)	48(41.7%)	7(6.1%)	
2.	Lack of low cost and accessible training facilities	57(50%)	44(38.6%)	13(11.4%)	1
3.	Lack of experience in owning/ managerial a business	56(49.6%)	51(45.1%)	6(5.3%)	2
4.	Lack of well trained & experienced employees in themarket	52(45.6%)	51(44.8%)	11(9.6%)	1
5.	Lack of clear division of activities and duties	44(38.6%)	56(49.2%)	14(12.2%)	1
6.	Dependence on family and relatives for labour	37(32.2%)	61(53.1%)	17(14.7%)	
7.	Personal problems (health, social) of owner/manager	46(40%)	51(44.3%)	18(15.7%)	
8.	High employee turnover	23(28.9%)	59(51.8%)	22(19.3%)	1

Source: Field survey.

From the above table it is seen that, the main managerial and HRM factors that affect the performance of MEs are lack of strategic business planning (52.2% agree, 41.7% disagree), lack of low cost and accessible training facilities (agree 50%, disagree 38.6%), lack of experience in owning/managing a business (agree 49.6%, disagree 45.1%), lack of well trained and experienced employees in the market (agree 45.6%, disagree 44.8%). Majority of the respondents disagreed on the other four problems like employee turnover, personal problem, dependence on family and relatives and lack of clear division of activities and duties.

Control and evaluation

Small businesses are characterised by lack of control and evaluation skill. Absence of proper raw material and inventory control measures impacts the production cost and selling price. Competitiveness and survival are possible only if MEs can provide quality product/services and achieve customer satisfaction.

Table - 12.5: Control and evaluation

S/N	*Control and evaluation*	*Agree*	*Disagree*	*I don't know*	*Missing*
1.	Over-emphasis on short term profitability	57(49.6%)	52(45.2%)	6(5.2%)	
2.	High family commitment and responsibility	60(47%)	47(40.8%)	8(7%)	
3.	Lack of quality control systems	42(36.5%)	55(47.8%)	18(15.7%)	
4.	Lack of raw material & inventory control	41(36.3%)	53(46.9%)	19(16.8%)	2
5.	Fear of failure, bankruptcy and risk taking	39(33.9%)	57(49.6%)	19(16.5%)	
6.	Lack of delegation responsibility and accountability	36(31.6%)	70(61.4%)	8(7%)	1

Source: Field survey.

Table-12.5 shows that 49.6 per cent of respondents agreed about over-emphasis on short term profitability, while 47 per cent of them agreed on high family commitment and responsibility. Although rural MEs fear of failure, bankruptcy and risk taking to take or evaluate loan and contract, only 33.9 agreed on the problem.

Recommendations

The nature of the problems identified in the study varies in complexity from sector to sector and region to region. These problems can be solved by the combined efforts of the MEs, NGOs and their stakeholders. Some recommendations in this regard are as follows:

- The designing and implementation of small business assistance programmes should be based on the identification and prioritisation of critical factors. Different problems with different degree of perceived impact on MEs can be addressed at different times in different ways depending on the availability of resources and situations in the operating environment.
- Most of the problems can be solved by designing effective and efficient business development services (BDS). Efforts must be made to incorporate entrepreneurship into the national culture and way of life. This calls for the integration of entrepreneurship with school curriculum starting from kindergarten. A network of agencies/institutions, both government and non- governmental,

providing a variety of services to promote and support entrepreneurship is very important.

- The DIC should improve its services - specially the business licence and company registration procedure. For this implementation of information technology with skilled manpower is crucial.
- In order to market the rural industries products, a common complex in every block, or at least in every district should be established by the DIC. Such solutions to the marketing problems of rural industries products would generate a large amount of income and employment potential in the rural areas.
- Support agencies should be given more autonomy so that they can act independently to simplify the stringent rules and regulations.
- A detailed study needs to be under taken on the site to be given, the people to be organised, the talent of the people and their capability of doing the intended business before giving the work place and licence.
- To solve the problem for finance for micro enterprises, the government should develop special loan system/strategy for micro enterprises with minimum collateral amount at fair interest rate. At the same time the government should support other informal sources to reduce the risk.
- Finally, the increase in the number of micro/small businesses in the district should not be equated with the development of entrepreneurship in the district. It is the development of entrepreneurship that leads to an increasing number of viable small firms, not vice versa.

Conclusion

In a nutshell, the study revealed that the rural entrepreneurs face problems of different magnitude during the course of setting up and managing their enterprises. Understanding the basic characteristics of rural areas and eliminating the inherent constraints of rural entrepreneurs can go a long way in framing proper policies for promoting and developing rural entrepreneurship.

BIBLOGRAPHY

Ahmed, S.U. (1985). nAch, Risk-taking Propensity, Locus of Control and Entrepreneurship, *Personality and Individual Differences*, *6* (6), 781-782. doi: https://doi.org/10.1016/0191-8869(85) 90092-3.

Akçomak, S. (2011). Incubators as Tools for Entrepreneurship Promotion in Developing Countries, *Entrepreneurship, Innovation, and Economic Development,* 228-264. doi: https://doi.org/10.1093/acprof:oso/9780199596515.003.0010.

Akhouri, M.M.P. (1979). Entrepreneurial Economic Success Index (EESI) for Assessing Entrepreneurial Success, *SEDME Journal*, 6(1), 36-49.

Alagappan, V., & Nagammai, R. (2003). Entrepreneurs Response to Financial Assistance from Institutions, *SEDME Journal*, 30(4), 25-32.

Aldrich, H., & Fiol, C. (1994). Fools Rush in? The Institutional Context of Industry Creation, *The Academy of Management Review, 19*(4), 645-670. Retrieved from http://www.jstor.org/stable/258740.

Amsden, A. (2011). Firm Ownership and Entrepreneurship, In A. Szirmai, W.A. Naudé and M. Goedhuys, eds., *Entrepreneurship, Innovation, and Economic Development,* Oxford: Oxford University Press, chapter-3.

Athreye, S. (2011). Overcoming Adversity in Entrepreneurship-led Growth, Evidence from the Indian Software Sector, *Entrepreneurship, Innovation, and Economic Development,* chapter-11.

Atkinson, J.W., & Walter, R.R. (1956). Performance as a function of motive strength and expectancy of goal-attainment, *Journal of abnormal psychology, 53*, 361-6. doi: https://doi.org/10.1037/h0043477.

Audretsch, D.B., Keilbach, M.C., & Lehman, E. (2006). Entrepreneurship and Economic Growth. New York, U.S.A.: *Oxford University Press,* ISBN-13: 9780195183511

Awasthi, A., Jaggi, & Padmanand V. (2004). A manual for entrepreneurs: Food Processing Industry.*Tata McGraw-Hill*, New Delhi.

Bandelj, N. (2016). On Post-Socialist Capitalism. Theory and Society, 45(1), 89-106, doi: https://doi.org/10.1007/s11186-016-9265-z accessed on 21 Sept 2016.

Bandelj, N., & Sowers, E., (2010). Economy and State: A Sociological Perspective, *Polity Press*. ISBN: 978-0-7456-4454-7, Retrieved from http://as.wiley.com/WileyCDA/WileyTitle/productCd-0745644546.html accessed on 21 Sept 2016.

Baron, R.A., & Markman, G.D. (2000). Beyond Social Capital: How Social Skills Can Enhance Entrepreneurs' Success, *The Academy of Management Executive* (1993-2005), *14*(1), 106-116. Retrieved from http://www.jstor.org/stable/4165612

Baron, R.A., & Markman, G.D. (2003). Beyond Social Capital: The Role of Entrepreneurs Social Competence in their Financial Success, *Journal of Business Venturing,* 18, 41-60. doi: https://doi.org/10.1016/S0883-9026(00) 00069-0

Barringer, and Ireland (2011). *Entrepreneurship: Successfully Launching New Ventures,* 3rd edition, New Delhi, India: Pearson.

Bascavusoglu-Moreau, E. (2011). Entrepreneurship and the National System of Innovation: What is Missing in Turkey? *Entrepreneurship, Innovation, and Economic Development,* chapter-7.

Bass, B.M. (1985). Leadership and Performance beyond Expectations. New York, N.Y.: *Free Press*.

Baumol, W.J. (2002). The Free-market Innovation Machine: Analyzing the Growth Miracle of Capitalism. Princeton: *Princeton University Press*.

Begley, T.M., Tan, W.L., & Schoch, H. (2005). Politico-Economic Factors Associated with Interest in Starting a Business: A Multi-Country Study. *Entrepreneurship Theory and Practice, 29*(1), 35-55, doi: 10.1111/j.1540-6520.2005.00068.x accessed on 20 Dec 2015.

Bender, G., & Hill, T.L. (2007). The Entrepreneurial Process: The Interplay of Social Competence, Opportunity Recognition and Success as an Entrepreneur, Paper presented at the United States of Association for Small Business and Entrepreneurship Conference.

Berglund, H. (2015). Between Cognition and Discourse: Phenomenology and the Study of Entrepreneurship. *International Journal of Entrepreneurial Behavior & Research, 21*(3), 472-488, doi: https://doi.org/10.1108/IJEBR-12-2013-0210 accessed on 20 Dec 2015.

Birch, D. (1987). Job Creation in America. New York: *Free Press.*

Bolino, M.C., & Turnley, W.H. (2003). More than One Way to Make an Impression: Exploring Profiles of Impression Management, *Journal of Management,* 29, 141-160. doi: https://doi.org/10.1016/S0149-2063(02)00212-X

Boyatzis, R. (1974). Affiliation Motivation. In D. McClelland and R. Steele (eds.), *Human* Motivation: A Book of Readings. Morristown, N.J.: *General Learning Press*, 252-76.

Brockhaus, R. (1980). Risk Taking Propensity of Entrepreneurs, *Academy of Management Journal.* 23, 509-20. Retrieved from http://www.jstor.org/stable/255515

Brush, C.G. (1997). Women-owned businesses: Obstacles and opportunities, *Journal of Developmental Entrepreneurship*, *2*(1), 1-24.

Buttner, E.H., & Rosen, B. (1988). Bank Loan Officer's Perceptions of the Characteristics of Men, Women and Successful Entrepreneurs, *Journal of Business Venturing*, *3*(3), 249-258. doi: https://doi.org/10.1016/0883-9026(88)90018-3

Buttner, E H., & Rosen, B. (1989). Funding New Business Ventures: Are Decision Makers biased against Women Entrepreneurs, *Journal of Business Venturing*, *4*(4), 249-261. doi: https://doi.org/10.1016/0883-9026(89)90015-3

Buttner, E.H., & Rosen, B. (1992). Rejection in the loan application process: Male and female entrepreneurs′perceptions and subsequent intentions, *Journal of Small Business Management*, *30*(1), 59-65.

Cable, D.M., & Shane, S. (1997). A Prisoner's Dilemma Approach to Entrepreneur-Venture Capitalist Relationships, *Academy of Management Review, 22*, 142-176. Retrieved from http://www.jstor.org/stable/259227

Caliendo, M., Fossen, F., & Kritikos, A. (2010). The Impact of Risk Attitudes on Entrepreneurial Survival, *Journal of Economic Behavior and Organization*, 76, 45-63. doi: https://doi.org/10.1016/j.jebo.2010.02.012

Carree, M.A., & Thurik, A.R. (2010). The Impact of Entrepreneurship on Economic Growth. In Acs', Z. J., Audretsch, D. B. (Ed.), *Handbook of Entrepreneurship Research*, 557-594, Springer: Science+Media: New York. doi: 10.1007/978-1-4419-1191-9_20, Retrieved from https://personal.eur.nl/thurik/Research/Articles/The%20impact%20of%20entrepreneurship%20 on%20economic%20growth%20-%20thurik%20chapter.pdf accessed on 20 Dec 2015.

Caldwell, D.F., & Burger, J.M. (1997). Personality and Social Influence Strategies in the Workplace. *Personality and Social Psychology Bulletin, 23*, 1003-1012. doi: https://doi.org/10.1177/01461672972310001.

Carland, J.W., Hoy, F., Boulton, W.R., & Carland, J.C. (1984). Differentiating Entrepreneurs from Small Business Owners: A Conceptualization, *Academy of Management Review*, 9 (2), 354-359. Retrieved from http://www.jstor.org/stable/258448

Carter, N.M., Williams, M., & Reynolds, P. D. (1997). Discontinuance among new firms in retail: The influence of initial resources, strategy, and gender, *Journal of Business Venturing*, 12(2), 125- 145. doi: https://doi.org/10.1016/S0883-9026(96)00033-X

Cefis E., & Marsili O. (2006). Survivor: the role of innovation in firm's survival. *Research Policy* 35, 626–641. doi: https://doi.org/10.1016/j.respol.2006.02.006

Cherrington D.J. (1989). *Organizational Behaviour.* Boston, MA: Allyn and Bacon.

Claiborne C.B. (2007). Innovation: A Necessity of the New Global Business Paradigm, *International Journal of Business Research,* N.V.:n.pp.

Covin, J.G., & Slevin, D.P. (1989). Strategic Management of Small Firms in Hostile and Benign Environments, *Strategic Management Journal, 10*(1), 75-88. doi: https://doi.org/10.1002/smj.4250100107

Cromie, S., & O'Sullivan, S. (1999). Women as Managers in Family Firms, *Women in Management Review, 14*(3), 76-88. doi: https://doi.org/10.1108/09649429910269884

Cunningham, J.B., & Lischeron, J. (1991). Defining Entrepreneurship, *Journal of Small Business Management, 29*(1), 45-61. Retrieved from https://www.questia.com/library/journal/1G1-10666908/defining-entrepreneurship

Cromie S. (2000). Assessing Entrepreneurial Inclinations: Some Approaches and Empirical Evidence, *European Journal of Work and Organizational Psychology,* 9, 7-30. doi: https://doi.org/10.1080/135943200398030.

Dagar, I. (2003). Industrial Relations in Small Scale Industry: A Study of Internal Factors, *Indian Journal of Commerce, 56*(1), 68-78.

Darby, B.W., & Schlenker, B.R. (1982). Children's Reactions to Apologies, *Journal of Personality and Social Psychology*, 43, 742-753. doi: http://dx.doi.org/10.1037/0022-3514.43.4.742

Department of Science and Technology, *Annual Report* 2013-14.

Dey, N.B., & Rahman, M. (2010). Micro and Small Enterprises in NE India: Problems & Prospects.*EBH Publishers*, Guwahati, 275-276, ISBN No.978-93-80261-00-3

Drucker P.F. (1999). Management's New Paradigms, *Management Challenges for the 21st Century,* New York: Harper Business, 1-41.

Drucker P.F. (1985). The Practice of Innovation, *Innovation and Entrepreneurship Practice and Principles,* New York: Harper & Row, 19-33.

Drucker P.F. (1985). The Practice of Entrepreneurship, Ibid., 141-88.

Drucker P.F. (1985). Entrepreneurial Strategies, Ibid., 207-43.

Dubey, A.R., & Shukla, O.P. (2007). Development of Small Scale Industries in India, *Indian Journal of Development Research and Social Action*, *3*(1), 49-57.

Eckhardt J.T., & Shane S.A. (2003). Opportunities and entrepreneurship.*Journal of management,* 29(3), 333-349. doi: https://doi.org/10.1016/S0149-2063(02)00225-8

Enterprises Report 2015, Kochi (Kerala). This is referred to as India MSME Report 2015.

Fairlie, R.W., & Holleran, W. (2012). Entrepreneurship Training, Risk Aversion and Other Personality Traits: Evidence from a Random Experiment, *Journal of Economic Psychology,* 33, 366-78. doi: https://doi.org/10.1016/j.joep.2011.02.001

Falbe, C.M., & Larwood, L. (1995). The Context of Entrepreneurial Vision, *Frontiers of Entrepreneurship Research*, Wellesley, Mass.: Babson College.

Feldman, M.S., & March, J.G. (1981). Information as a Signal and Symbol, *Administrative Science Quarterly*, 26(2), 171-186. doi: https://doi.org/10.2307/2392467

Fiske, S.T., & Taylor, S.E. (1991). Social Cognition (2nd edn.), New York: *McGraw-Hill.*

Fridlund, A.J., Sabini, J.P., Hedlund, L.E., Schaut, J.A., Shenker, J.L., & Knauer, M.J. (1990). Social determinants of facial expressions during affective imagery: Displaying to the people in your head, *Journal of Nonverbal Behavior*, *14*, 113–137.

Fridlund, A. J. (1991). The Sociality of Solitary Smiles: Effects of an Implicit Audience, *Journal of Personality and Social Psychology*, 60, 229-240.

Formaini, R.L. (2001). The engine of capitalist process: Entrepreneurs in economic theory, *Economic & Financial Review*, 2.

Gallagher, V.C. (2007). Situational and Dispositional Antecedents and Consequences of Impression Management Tactics: The Role of Political Skill, Florida State University. Retrieved from http://purl.flvc.org/fsu/fd/FSU_migr_etd-4381

Gangestad, S.W., & Snyder, M. (2000). Self-monitoring: Appraisal and Reappraisal, *Psychological Bulletin*, 126, 530-555. doi: https://doi.org/10.1037/0033-2909.126.4.530.

Gartner W.B. (1990). What are we Talking about when we Talk about Entrepreneurship? *Journal of Business Venturing*, 5, 15-28. doi: https://doi.org/10.1016/0883-9026(90)90023-M

Geetha, N., & Govindappa, T.G. (2011). Socio-Economic Background and Problems of Entrepreneurs in Industrial Estate: A Case Study of Industrial Estate in Davangere, *SEDME Journal, 38*(3), 1-41, retrieved from http://ojs.nimsme.org/index.php/Document1/issue/view/26 accessed on 23 Sept 2011

Glaub, M. (2009). Training Personal Initiative to Business Owners in Developing Countries; A Theoretically Derived Intervention and Its Evaluation, Ph.D dissertatory, Justus- Liebig University, Gieben, Germany.

Glaub, M., & Frese, M. (2011). A Critical Review of the Effects of Entrepreneurship Training in Developing Countries, *Enterprise Development & Microfinance,* 22, 335-53. Indian express.com November 13, 2015. New Delhi. doi: https://doi.org/10.3362/1755-1986.2011.035.

Godfrey, D.K., Jones, E.E., & Lord, C.G. (1986). Self-promotion is Not Ingratiating, *Journal of Personality and Social Psychology*, 50, 106-115. doi: https://doi.org/10.1037/0022-3514.50.1.106.

Goffman, E. (1963). *Stigma: Notes on the Management of Spoiled Identity,* Englewood Cliffs, NJ: Prentice-Hall.

Gupta, R., Sankhe S., Dobbs, R., Woetzel, J., Madgavkar A., & Hasyagar, A. (2014). From Poverty to Empowerment: India's Growth Imperative for Jobs, Growth, and Effective Basic Services, McKinsey & Company, Retrieved from http://www.mckinsey.com/insights/asiapacific/indias_path_from_poverty_to_empowerment, accessed August 2017.

Hair, J.F., Black, W.C., Babin, B.J., & Andeson R.E. (2010). Multivariate Data Analysis, 7th Edition, *Pearson Publication.* ISBN: 0135153093.

Hannafey, F.T. (2003). Entrepreneurship and ethics: A Literature Review.*Journal of Business Ethics,* 46(2), 99-110.

Hayton, J.C., George, G., & Zahra, S.A. (2002). National Culture and Entrepreneurship: A Review of Behavioral Research, *Entrepreneurship: Theory and Practice*, 26(4), 33-53. doi: https://doi.org/10.1177/104225870202600403

Hedayatullah Chowdhury, Md. (2000). Performance of Small Entrepreneurs - The Case of Dholai-Khal, *SEDME Journal*, June, 27(2), 1-24.

Hindle, K. (2010). How Community Context Affects Entrepreneurial Process: A Diagnostic Framework. *Entrepreneurship & Regional Development, 22*(7-8), 599-647, doi: http://dx.doi.org/10.1080/08985626.2010.522057 accessed on 22 Dec 2015.

Hisrich, R.D., & Jancowicz, A.D. (1990). Intuition in Venture Capital Decisions: An Exploratory Study Using a New Technique, *Journal of Business Venturing*, *5*(1), 49-62. doi: https://doi.org/10.1016/0883-9026(90)90026-P

Holland, J.L. (1985). Making Vocational Choices: A Theory of Vocational Personalities and Work Environments (2nd edn.), Odessa, FL: Psychological Assessment Resources.

Hornaday, & Aboud (1971). Cited in J.W. Carland, F. Hoy, W.R. Boulton and J.C. Carland (1984). Differentiating Entrepreneurs from Small Business Owners: A Conceptualization, *Academy of Management Review*, *9*, 354-359.

Hossain, S., & Uddin, M.A. (2006). Problems in Financing and Managing Small-Scale Enterprises in Bangladesh: An Empirical Study on Some Rural Areas of Chittagong and Cox's Bazar. *The Social Sciences, 1,* 22-28. Retrieved from http://medwelljournals.com/abstract/?doi=sscience.2006.22.28 accessed on 05 Mar 2010.

House, R.J. (1977). A 1976 Theory of Charismatic Leadership. In J.G. Hunt and L.L. Larson (Eds.). Leadership: The Cutting Edge. Carbondale, IL: *Southern Illinois University Press*, 189-207.

Huggins, R., & Williams, N. (2011). Entrepreneurship and Regional Competitiveness: The Role and Progression of Policy. *Entrepreneurship & Regional Development, 23*(9-10), 907-932. doi: http://dx.doi.org/10.1080/08985626.2011.577818 accessed on 22 Dec 2015.

India. Department of Industrial Policy and Promotion (DIPP), Ministry of Commerce and Industry, GoI (2016), Action Plan – StartupIndia, January 16, 2016, New Delhi.

India. Department of Science and Technology (DST), Ministry of Science and Technology (2016), Annual Report 2015-16, New Delhi.

India. Ministry of MSME (2012), Report of the Working Group on MSMEs Growth for 12th Five Year Plan (2012-17), New Delhi.

India. Ministry of MSME (2016), Annual Report 2015-16, New Delhi.

Institute of Small Enterprises and Development (ISED) (2015), India Micro, Small and Medium Ismail, A.Z., Zain, M.F.B.M, & Ahmed, E.M. (2006). A Study of Motivation in Business Start-Ups Among Malay Entrepreneurs, *International Business & Economics Research Journal (IBER), 5*(2), 103-112. doi: http://dx.doi.org/10.19030/iber.v5i2.3462.

Jain, R.K., Jain, R., & Triandis, H.C. (1997). Management of Research and Development Organizations: Managing the Unmanageable, 2nd edn, New York: John Wiley & Sons. ISBN: 9780471146131

Jones, E.E., Pittman, T.S., & Jones, E.E. (1982). Toward a General Theory of Strategic Self-Presentation. In: Suls, J., Ed., *Psychological Perspectives on the Self, 1*, Erlbaum, Hillsdale, 231-262.

Joshi, G. (2001). Entrepreneurship Development for SMEs in the 21st Century, *Productivity*, 42(2), 186-190.

Kar, B., Mishra, R., & Mohanty, J. (2014). Revisiting the Factors Influencing Entry and Success of Entrepreneurship, *The International Journal of Management,* 3(3), 34-47. Available at SSRN: https://ssrn.com/abstract=2533106 or http://dx.doi.org/10.2139/ssrn.2533106

Kazmi, A. (1999). What Young Entrepreneurs Think and Do: A Study of Second Generation Business Entrepreneurs, *The Journal of Entrepreneurship*, 8(1), 68.

Khanka, S.S. (2009). Motivational Orientation of Assamese Entrepreneurs in the SME Sector. *The Journal of Entrepreneurship, 18*(2), 209 – 218. doi:10.1177/097135570901800204

Kipnis, D., Schmidt, S.M., & Wilkinson, I. (1980). Intra-organizational Influence Tactics: Explorations in Getting One's Way, *Journal of Applied Psychology*, *65*, 440-452. doi: http://dx.doi.org/10.1037/0021-9010.65.4.440

Kirton, M. (1976). Adaptors and innovators: A description and measure, *Journal of Applied Psychology, 61*(5), 622–629. doi: http://dx.doi.org/10.1037/0021-9010.61.5.622.

Knight, F.H. (1921). Risk, Uncertainty and Profit, Chicago: *University of Chicago Press*.

Koenig, B.L. & Nezlek, J.B. (2004). Evolutionary Psychology of Impression Management: Mating Strategies in Everyday Interactions, *Human Behavior and Evolution Society Annual Meeting*, Berlin, Germany.

Koh, H.C. (1996). Testing Hypothesis of Entrepreneurial Characteristics, A Study of Hong Kong MBA Students. *Journal of Managerial Psychology, 11*(3), 12-25. doi: https://doi.org/10.1108/02683949610113566

Krippner, G., & Alvarez, A. (2007). Embeddedness and the Intellectual Projects of Economic Sociology. *Annual Review of Sociology, 33*, 219–240, doi: https://doi.org/10.1146/ annurev.soc.33.040406.131647 accessed on 22 Dec 2015.

Kumar, J. & Lalthunthara (2012). Socio-Economic Background of Micro Entrepreneurs in Aizwal District, Mizoram. *SEDME Journal, 39*(2), 1-17, Retrieved from http://ojs.nimsme.org/index.php/ Document1/issue/view/32 accessed on 22 Jul 2012

Kuruba, G. (2006). Issues in Promotion of Small Business Enterprises in Botswana. *Indian Journal of Commerce, 59*(1), 77-86.

Laghu Udyog Samachar, *41*(6), *41*(11) & *41*(12), January, June & July, *42*(1), August 2016 – *Monthly Journal of Development Commissioner (MSME)*, New Delhi. www.dcmsme.gov.in

Leary, M.R., & Kowalski, R.M. (1990). Impression Management: A Literature Review and Two-component Model, *Psychological Bulletin*, 107, 34-47. doi: https://doi.org/10.1037/0033-2909.107.1.34.

Lipsey, R.G., Carlaw, K.I., & Bekar, C.T. (2005). *Economic Transformations: General Purpose Technologies and Long-Term Economic Growth.* Oxford: Oxford University Press.

Long, W. (1983). The Meaning of Entrepreneurship, *American Journal of Small Business,* 8, 47-56.

Longenecker, J.G., McKinney, J.A., & Moore, C.W. (1989). Egoism and independence: Entrepreneurial ethics. *Organizational Dynamics*, *16*(3), 64-72. doi: https://doi.org/10.1016/0090-2616(88)90037-X

Low, M.B., & Macmillan, I.C. (1988). Entrepreneurship: Past Research and Future Challenges, *Journal of Management*, *14*(2), 139-161. doi: https://doi.org/10.1177/014920638801400202

Lumpkin, G.T., & Dess, G.G. (1996). Clarifying the Entrepreneurial Orientation Construct and Linking It to Performance, *The Academy of Management Review, 21*(1), 135-172. doi: https://doi.org/10.2307/258632

Macmillan, I.C., Block, Z., & Narashimha, P.N.S. (1985). Corporate Venturing: Alternatives, Obstacles Encountered, and Experience Effects, *Journal of Business Venturing, 1*(2), 177-191. doi: https://doi.org/10.1016/0883-9026(86)90013-3

Mambula (2002). Perceptions of SMEs Growth Constraints in Nigeria, *Journal of Small Business Management*, *40*(1), 58-65. doi: https://doi.org/10.1111/1540-627X.00039

Mani, S. (2011). Promoting Knowledge-intensive Entrepreneurship in India, *Entrepreneurship,Innovation, and Economic Development,* chapter-9.

Marlow, S. (1997). Self-employed women - new opportunities, old challenges? *Entrepreneurship and Regional Development*, *9*(3), 199-210. doi: https://doi.org/10.1080/08985629700000011

Martínez, A.C., Levie, J., Kelley, D.J., Saemundsson, R.J., & Schott, T. (2010). A Global Perspective on Entrepreneurship Education and Training, GEM Report (online). http://www.gemconsortium.org (accessed 12 May 2010).

Mason, C., & Harrison, R. (2000). Auditioning for Money: What Do Investors Look for at the Initial Screening Stage?, In R.D. Hisrich and E. Hacker (eds.), *Proceedings of the Entrepreneurial Finance Workshop*, Jonkoping, Sweden: Jonkoping International Business School, 155-176.

Match, D. (1991). Quoted in Exploring Entrepreneurial Orientation (EO) in 3 Dimensions: A New Prospective for Analyzing the Value of a Company by Zhan Jun and Dirk Deschoolmeester (2007).

Malathi, V.G. (2005). Role Conflicts of Women Entrepreneurs, Indian Institute of Management, NISIET, Government of India, Hyderabad, Page No. 54 to 55.

McClelland, D.C. (1965). Achievement Motivation Can be Developed, *Harvard Business Review*, *43*, 6-24.

McClelland, D.C. (1953). The Achievement Society, New York: Appleton, *Martino Fine Books*. ISBN-13: 978-1891396397

McDaniel, B.A. (2005). A Contemporary View of Joseph A. Schumpeter's theory of the Entrepreneur. *Journal of Economic Issues*, *39*(2), 485-489. Retrieved from http://www.jstor.org/stable/4228161

Mead, D.C., & Liedholm, C. (1998). The Dynamics of Micro and Small Enterprises in Developing Countries, *World Development, 26*(1), 61-74. doi: https://doi.org/10.1016/S0305-750X(97)10010-9

Medha, D.V. (1987). Women Entrepreneurs in India, Mittal Publications, New Delhi, Page No. 110 to 112.

Meek, W.R., Pacheco, D.F., & York, J.G. (2010). The Impact of Social Norms on Entrepreneurial Action: Evidence from the Environmental Entrepreneurship Context. *Journal of Business Venturing, 25*(5), 493-509, doi: https://doi.org/10.1016/j.jbusvent.2009.09.007 accessed on 24 Dec 2015.

Mehta, A. & Mehta, M. C., (Dec-2011). Rural Women Entrepreneurship in India opportunities and challenges, *International Conference on Humanities, Geography and Economics*, (ICHGE) Pattaya, Page No - 313-315. Retrieved from psrcentre.org/images/extraimages/40.%201211306.pdf

Meti, S.K. (2013). Social And Economic Empowerment of Farm Women in Agro based Entrepreneurship for Sustainable Income. Proceeding *of the International Conference on Social Science Research*, Penang, Malyasia, ICSSR 2013 (e-ISBN 978-967- 11768-1-8). 4-5.

Miller, D. (1983). The Correlates of Entrepreneurship in Three Types of Firms, *Management Science*, 29, 770–791. Retrieved from http://www.jstor.org/stable/2630968

Miner, J.B., & Raju, N.S. (2004). Risk Propensity Differences between Managers and Entrepreneurs and between Low- and High-growth Entrepreneurs: A Reply in a More Conservative Vein, *Journal of Applied Psychology*, 89, 3-13. doi: https://doi.org/10.1037/0021-9010.89.1.3.

Ministry of Small Scale Industries and Agro & Rural Industries, (2000). Annual Report of Small Scale Industries. New Delhi: Government of India.

Mowday, R.T. (1978). The Exercise of Upward Influence in Organizations, *Administrative Science Quarterly*, *23*(1), 137-156. doi: https://doi.org/10.2307/2392437

Mowday, R.T., Steers, R.M., & Porter, L.W. (1979). The Measurement of Organizational Commitment, *Journal of Vocational Behavior, 14*(2), 224-47. doi: https://doi.org/10.1016/0001-8791(79)90072-1

MSMED Act 2006, Ministry of Small Scale Industries, Notification, July 18, 2006, Government of India. Naude, W. (2011). Entrepreneurship and Economic Development. New York, U.S.A.: New York: NY: *Palgrave Macmillan,* ISBN: 978-1-349-32809-3.

Niti Aayog, (2015). Report of the Expert Committee on Innovation and Entrepreneurship. Retrieved from niti.gov.in/documents/reports/Report of the Expert Committee on Innovation and Entrepreneurship accessed on 8-11-2016.

Nithyananan, R . (21-22 June, 2008). Development of Island Fisheries, *ICAR and NABARD*, Port Blair, A & N Islands, Page No. 1 – 4.

Olson, P. (1986). Entrepreneurs: Opportunistic Decision Makers, *Journal of Small Business Management,* 24(3), 29-35.

Padmanand, V., Reddy, M.C., Satyaprakash, T.L., & Sood, K. (2016). Rise of the Third World: In the enabling policy and regulatory environment. *Small Enterprises Development, Management and Extension Journal, 43*(1).

Padmanand, V., & Kurian, P.H. (2014). Rise of Indian Industry. Kerala Bureau for Industrial Promotion, Govt. of Kerala, Thiruvananthapuram.

Padmanand, V., & Vinanchiarachi, J. (2008). Intervene to industrialise: A holistic approach to enabling business environment, entrepreneurship and cluster value chain development. Kerala Bureau for Industrial Promotion, Govt. of Kerala, Thiruvananthapuram.

Padmanand, V., & Kurian, P.H. (2009). Entrepreneurship in Developing Countries, Kerala Bureau for Industrial Promotion, Govt. of Kerala, Thiruvananthapuram.

Padmanand, V., & Gulati, M. (2006). Interventionary instruments for cluster development. *Allied Publishers*, Hyderabad.

Padmanand, V., & Patel, V.G. (2004). Managing India's Small Industrial Economy.*Sage Publications*, New Delhi.

Padmanand, V., & Jain, P.C. (1999). Doing Business in India: Street-smart Entrepreneurs in an Imperfect Marketplace; *Sage Publications*, New Delhi.

Pandian, P., & Eswaran.R. (Nov 2002). Empowerment of Women Through Micro–Credit, *Yojana*, 46 (11), Page No. 47 -49.

Paulhus, D.L. (1984). Two Component Model of Socially Desirable Responding, *Journal of Personality and Social Psycholog*, 46, 598-609. doi: http://dx.doi.org/10.1037/0022-3514.46.3.598

Paulhus, D.L., Harms, P.D., Bruce, M.N., & Lysy, D.C. (2003). The Over-claiming Technique: Measuring Self-enhancement Independent of Ability, *Journal of Personality and Social*

Psychology, *84*(4), 890-904. doi: http://dx.doi.org/10.1037/0022-3514.84.4.890

Peluchette, J.V., Karl, K.A., & Rust, K. (2006). Dressing to Impress: Belief and Attitudes and Attitudes Regarding Workplace Attire, *Journal of Business and Psychology, 21*(1), 45-63. Retrieved from http://www.jstor.org/stable/25473469

Permal, S.V. : Rural Entrepreneurship & Rural Development, Entrepreneurship and Small Business Development, in Batra, G.S & Bhaktia G.S. (Eds), Entrepreneurship & Small Business Management, *Deep & Deep Publications*, New Delhi, 2000, 69-78.

Perrewé, P.L., & Spector, P.E. (2002). Personality Research in the Organizational Sciences, *Research in Personnel and Human Resources Management*, 21, 1-64. *Emerald Group Publishing Limited,* 1 – 63. Retrieved from https://www.emeraldinsight.com/doi/abs/10.1016/S0742-7301%2802%2921001-4

Pontari, B.A., & Schlenker, B.R. (2000). The Influence of Cognitive Load on Self-presentation: Can Cognitive Busyness Help as Well as Harm Social Performance? *Journal of Personality and Social Psychology, 78(*6), 1092-108. http://dx.doi.org/10.1037//0022-3514.78.6.1092.

Ramalaingam, C., & Gayatri, R. (2006). A Framework for Development of Rural Entrepreneurship in Tamilnadu Using Innovation as Strategic Tool, retrieved from http://www.indianmba.com/ Faculty_Column/FC995/fc995.html accessed on 13 Mar 2010.

Rasiah, R., Vinanchiarachi, J., & Padmanand, V. (2014). Catching-Up from Way Behind: How Timor- Leste Can Avoid the Dutch Disease? *Institutions and Economies, 6*(1), 119-14. Retrieved from https://ijie.um.edu.my/index.php/ijie/article/view/4922.

Richard, O.C., Barnett, T., Dwyer, S., & Chadwick, K. (2004). Cultural Diversity in Management, Firm Performance, and the Moderating Role of Entrepreneurial Orientation Mechanisms, *Academy of Management Journal, 47*(2), 255-266. Retrieved from https://misweb.business.msstate.edu/~COBI/faculty/users/tbarnett/AMJ2004.pdf

Riding, A.L., & Swift, C.S. (1990). Women business owners and terms of credit: Some empirical findings of the Canadian Experience, *Journal of Business Venturing, 5*(5), 327-340. doi: https://doi.org/10.1016/0883-9026(90)90009-I

Roberts, E.B. (1968). Entrepreneurship and Technology: A Basic Study of Innovators, *Research Management, 11*(4), 249-66. doi: https://doi.org/10.1080/00345334.1968.11755911

Rosenfeld, P., Giacalone, R.A. & Riordan, C.A. (1995). *Impression Management in Organizations: Theory, Measurement, Practice.* London: *Routledge*. ISBN: 9780415126793

Rosenfeld, P., Giacalone, R.A. & Riordan, C.A. (2002). Impression Management: Building and Enhancing Reputations at Work, London: *Thomson Learning*. ISBN: 9781861529701

Santana, K.R., & Jegadeesan, G. (2008). Entrepreneurship and Rural Development in India, *ICFAI University Press*, Hyderabad, 7, ISBN: 978-81-314-1428-6.

Schlenker, B.R., & Weigold, M.F. (1992). Interpersonal Processes Involving Impression Regulation and Management, *Annual Review of Psychology, 43*(1), 133-168. doi: https://doi.org/10.1146/annurev.ps.43. 020192. 001025

Schneider, D.J. (1981). Tactical Self-presentations: Toward a Broader Conception. In J.T. Tedeschi (ed.), *Impression Management Theory and Social Psychological Research*, New York: Academic Press Inc., 23-40.

Schonbach, P. (1980). A Category System for Account Phases, *European Journal of Social Psychology, 10*(2), 195-200. doi: http://dx.doi.org/10.1002/ejsp.2420100206

Schrank, A. (2015). Toward a New Economic Sociology of Development. *Sociology of Development, 1*(2), 25–50, doi: 10.1525/sod.2015.1.2.25 accessed on 24 Nov 2015.

Schumpeter, J.A. (1911). The Theory of Economic Development: An Inquiry into Profits, Capital, Credit, Interest, and the Business Cycle, Harvard Economic Studies 46, 1-255. ISBN 9780674879904

Seshagiri, B., Satyavthi, C., & Sravanthi, Y. (2014). A study on women entrepreneurship in Non-Descript Rural Fish Markets. *Global Journal for Research Analysis International*, Social Sciences, 3(8), August special issue, ISSN No.2277-8160, Page No. 1 - 4

Shane, S., & Venkataraman, S. (2000). The Promise of Entrepreneurship as a Field of Research, *Academy of Management Review, 25*(1), 217-226. Retrieved from http://www.jstor.org/stable/259271

Sharma, V. (2017). A Study of Employment Preferences with Special Reference to Entrepreneurship Among the Educated Youth of Jammu and Kashmir (India). Katra, S.M.V.D University. Doctoral dissertation.

Sharma, Y. (Nov-Dec. 2013). Women Entrepreneuir in India, *IOSR Journal of Business and Management* (IOSR-JBM).15(3), Page No.09-14. e-ISSN: 2278-487X, P-ISSN: 2319- 7668

Singh, M.B., & Namboodiri, N.V.K. (2006). Unleashing Rural Entrepreneurship, *ICFAI University Press*, Hyderabad, 4, ISBN no.81-314-0573-7.

Sinha, H. (2010). Block Administration Without Panchayat Raj Institutions: An Assessment into the Lunglei District of Mizoram, *Kurukshetra, 58*(12), 44-47, retrieved from http://yojana.gov.in/CMS/(S(y4dqrc55g1m1qhnd4soqih45))/pdf/Kurukshetra/English/2010/October.pdf accessed on 03 Apr 2011

Small Industries Development Bank of India (SIDBI), Annual Report 2015-16, Lucknow.

Snyder, M. (1974). Self-monitoring of Expressive Behavior, *Journal of Personality and Social Psychology,* 30, 526-537. doi: http://dx.doi.org/10.1037/h0037039

Stam, E., & van Stel, A. (2011). Types of Entrepreneurship and Economic Growth, *Entrepreneurship, Innovation, and Economic Development,* chapter- 4.

Staniszkis, J. (1991). The Dynamics of Breakthrough. Berkeley, California.: *University of California Press.* ISBN: 9780520072183.

Steers, R.M., & Braunstein, D.N. (1976). A Behaviorally-based Measure of Manifest Needs in Work Settings, *Journal of Vocational Behavior, 9*(2), 251-266. doi: https://doi.org/10.1016/0001-8791(76)90083-X

Stel, A.V. (2006). *Empirical Analysis of Entrepreneurship and Economic Growth*, International Studies in Entrepreneurship Series, 13, New York: Springer Science. doi: https://doi.org/10.1007/0-387-29419-8

Stevenson, H.H., & Jarillo, J.C. (1990). A Paradigm of Entrepreneurship: Entrepreneurial Management, *Strategic Management Journal*, 11, 17-27. Retrieved from http://www.jstor.org/stable/2486667

Stewart, Jr., W.H., & Roth, P.L. (2001). Risk Propensity Differences between Entrepreneurs and Managers: A Meta-analytic Review, *Journal of Applied Psychology, 86*(1), 145-53. doi: https://doi.org/10.1037/0021-9010.86.1.145

Stiglitz, J. (2000). Whither Reform? Ten years of Transition. In B. Pleskovic, & J. Stiglitz (Eds.), Annual World Bank Conference on Economic Development, 127–171, Washington, D.C.: World Bank.

Supriya, M.V., & Srinath, T.T. (2003). Perception of Small Scale Entrepreneurs in Tamilnadu Regarding Successful and Unsuccessful Qualities of Entrepreneurs, *SEDME Journal*, 30(3), 31-49.

Swann, W.B. (1996). *Self-traps: The Elusive Quest for Higher Self-esteem,* New York: Freeman.

Szirmai, A., Naudé, W., & Goedhuys, M. (2011). Entrepreneurship, Innovation, and Economic Development.: *Oxford University Press.* Retrieved from http://www.oxfordscholarship.com/view/10.1093/acprof:oso/9780199596515.001.0001/acprof-9780199596515 accessed on 24 Nov 2015.

Tagoe, N., Nyarko, E., & AnuwaAmarh, E. (2005). Financial Challenges Facing Urban SMEs under Financial Sector Liberalisation in Ghana, *Journal of Small Business Management, 43*(3), 331-343. doi: https://doi.org/10.1111/j.1540-627X.2005.00140.x

Taylor, & Brooksbank (1995). Marketing Practices among Small New Zealand Organisations, *Journal of Enterprising Culture, 3*(2), 149-160.

Tedeschi (1984). A Social Psychological Interpretation of Human Aggression, In *Social Psychology of Aggression.* A. Mummendi (ed) Berlin : Springer-Verlag.

Toma, S.J., Grigore, A.M., & Marinescu, P. (2014). Economic Development and Entrepreneurship. *Procedia Economics and Finance. 8,* 436–443, doi: https://doi.org/10.1016/S2212- 5671(14)00111-7 accessed on 24 Nov 2015.

Trettin, L., & Welter, F. (2011). Challenges for Spatially Oriented Entrepreneurship Research. *Entrepreneurship and Regional Development, 23*, 575-602, doi: http://dx.doi.org/ 10.1080/08985621003792988 accessed on 14 Dec 2015.

Urbanaviciute, I., Poiciute, B., Kairys, A., & Liniauskaite, A. (2016). Perceived Career Barriers and Vocational Outcomes among University Graduates: Exploring Mediation and Moderation Effects. *Journal of Vocational Behaviour, 92*, 12-21, doi: http://dx.doi.org/10.1016/j.jvb.2015.11.001 accessed on 14 Dec 2015.

Venkataraman, S. (1997). The Distinctive Domains of Entrepreneurship Research: An Editor's Perspective. In J. Katz and R. Brockhaus (ed.), Advances in Entrepreneurship, Firm Emergence and Growth, 3, 119-138, Greenwich, CT: *JAI Press.*

Venkatasubramanian, V., Sanjeev, M.V., & Singha, A.K. (2009). Concepts, Approaches and Methodologies for Technology Application and Transfer – A Resource Book for KVKs, Umiam, Meghalaya, India: Indian Council of Agricultural Research.

Wadhwa V., Aggarwal, R., Holly, K.Z., & Salkever, A. (2009). The Anatomy of an Entrepreneur-Making of a Successful Entrepreneur, Research funded by the Ewing Marion Kauffman Foundation, Kansas City M.O., USA. doi: http://dx.doi.org/10.2139/ssrn.1507384

Wainer, H.A., & Rubin, I.M. (1969). Motivation of Research and Development Entrepreneurs: Determinants of Company Success, *Journal of Applied Psychology*, *53*(3), 178-84. doi: http://dx.doi.org/10.1037/h0027414

Walzer, N. (2009). Entrepreneurship and Local Economic Development, Lanham: *Lexington Books,* ISBN: 0739117122, 9780739117125

Wayne, W.J., & Kacmar, K. (1991). The Effects of Impression Management on the Performance Appraisal Process, *Organizational Behavior and Human Decision Processes*, *48*(1), 70-88. doi: https://doi.org/10.1016/0749-5978(91)90006-F

Witt, L.A., Kacmar, K.M., Carlson, D.S., & Zivnuska, S. (2002). Interactive Effects of Personality and Organizational Politics on Contextual Performance, *Journal of Organizational Performance*, *23*(8), 911-926. doi: https://doi.org/10.1002/job.172

Wu, J., Song, J., & Zeng, C. (2008). An Empirical Evidence of Small Business Financing in China, *Management Research News*, 31(12), 959-975. doi: https://doi.org/10.1108/01409170810920666

Yukl, G., & Falbe, C.M. (1990). Influence Tactics and Objectives in Upward, Downward, and Lateral influence Attempts, *Journal of Applied Psychology,* *75*(2), 132-140. doi: http://dx.doi.org/10.1037/0021-9010.75.2.132

Zeffane, R. (2014). Does Collectivism Necessarily Negate the Spirit of Entrepreneurship? *International Journal of Entrepreneurial Behavior & Research,* *20*(3), 278-296, doi: https://doi.org/10.1108/IJEBR-03-2013-0042 accessed on 14 Dec 2015.

Index